THE GREAT FILLING STATION HOLDUP

THE GREAT FILLING STATION HOLDUP

Crime Fiction Inspired
by the Songs of
Jimmy Buffett

JOSH PACHTER, EDITOR

DOWN&OUT
BOOKS

Down & Out Books
3959 Van Dyke Road, Suite 265
Lutz, FL 33558
DownAndOutBooks.com

The characters and events in this book are fictitious. Any similarity to real persons, living or dead, is coincidental and not intended by the author.

Cover design by Zach McCain

ISBN: 1-64396-181-0
ISBN-13: 978-1-64396-181-1

TABLE OF CONTENTS

To Parrotheads everywhere:
We're growing older, but not up...

INTRODUCTION

When his *One Particular Harbour* album was released in 1983, Jimmy Buffett was thirty-six years old, and I had just turned thirty-two. Today, as I write these words, he is seventy-three and I am sixty-eight. Jimmy's mother and father died a few months apart in 2003, mine are still alive and in their nineties—and I think it'd probably be accurate to say, as Jimmy sang on the album, that we really *are* the people our parents warned us about.

James William Buffett was born in Pascagoula, Mississippi, on December 25, 1946, a Christmas Day gift to his parents, James Delaney Buffett Jr., and Mary Louise Buffett. He spent his childhood and young-adult years in Mississippi and Alabama, earned a B.A. in history from the University of Southern Mississippi in 1969, and released his first LP, *Down to Earth*, on Barnaby Records a year later. Although his debut didn't chart, it led to a contract with ABC Records, which put out six Buffett albums between 1973's *A White Sport Coat and a Pink Crustacean* and 1978's *Son of a Son of a Sailor*. His 1977 release—*Changes in Attitudes, Changes in Latitudes*—went to #2 on the country charts in the U.S., #7 on the pop charts. (By the way, James Delaney Buffett Sr., it should perhaps be noted, was a sailor, making Jimmy in actual fact—no fake news here!—the son of a son of a sailor...)

Between 1979 and 1989, MCA Records put out nine Buffett albums; the most successful were the first, *Volcano* (1979),

1

which peaked at #13 on the country charts and #14 on the pop charts, and the sixth, *Last Mango in Paris* (1985), which made it up to #7 on the country charts.

And so Jimmy went on, "quietly, quietly, quietly making noise," with three releases on Margaritaville/MCA, then two on Margaritaville/Island, one on Mailboat, two on Mailboat/RCA Nashville, and three more back on Mailboat, taking us right up to last year's *Life on the Flip Side*.

That's a total of twenty-eight albums in fifty years, the most successful being 2004's *License to Chill*, which hit #1 on both the country *and* pop charts and was certified platinum by the Recording Industry Association of America. Quite a career— and that's not even counting the novels (such as *A Salty Piece of Land* and *Where is Joe Merchant?*), the memoirs (*Tales from Margaritaville* and *A Pirate Looks at Fifty*), the children's books (*The Jolly Mon* and *Trouble Dolls*, co-authored with Savannah Jane Buffett, Jimmy's daughter), and the stage show (*Don't Stop the Carnival*, based on the novel by Herman Wouk).

Last year, I edited an anthology titled *The Beat of Black Wings: Crime Fiction Inspired by the Songs of Joni Mitchell*. The book—published by Untreed Reads—sold well, with a third of the royalties going to the Brain Aneurysm Foundation. I had a great time editing it and decided to do a similar collection based on Buffett's songs. This time around, I concentrated on Florida authors, and about half of the writers represented in these pages call the Sunshine State their home. As with *The Beat of Black Wings*, a third of the royalties generated by the sales of this volume will go to charity—in this case equally divided between the Save the Manatee Club and Singing for Change.

The Save the Manatee Club was co-founded in 1981 by Jimmy and former Florida governor Bob Graham. Its mission is to "help protect manatees and their aquatic habitat for future generations by aiding in the recovery and protection of manatees and their aquatic ecosystems throughout the world." You can read about their work at *savethemanatee.org*.

Singing for Change is a private foundation Jimmy set up in 1995 to support organizations that inspire personal growth and community integration, and enhance awareness to allow people, collectively, to bring about positive social change. Read more about the foundation at *singingforchange.org*.

Save the Manatee Club and Singing for Change are two great causes doing great work in the world. Hmm, since Jimmy created them, and the authors who wrote the stories you're about to read are donating a significant portion of their royalties to supporting them, maybe the truth is that we are the people our parents *wanted* us to be...

We hope you enjoy these stories, inspired by the lyrics of one of the world's great storytellers.

Shake it up, baby!

Josh Pachter
Midlothian, Virginia
January 30, 2021

Down to Earth
Released 1970

"The Christian?"
"Ellis Dee (He Ain't Free)"
"The Missionary"
"A Mile High in Denver"
"The Captain and the Kid"
"Captain America"
"Ain't He a Genius"
"Turnabout"
"There's Nothin' Soft About Hard Times"
"I Can't Be Your Hero Today"
"Truckstop Salvation"

All songs by Jimmy Buffett,
except "The Christian?" (with Milton Brown)
and "Ellis Dee (He Ain't Free)" (with Buzz Cason).

TRUCKSTOP SALVATION

Leigh Lundin

1978

Barely squeezing under the max eighteen-foot clearance where Greyhounds feared to tread, the hugest motorhome this town ever saw crept across the rusty McAllister Bridge. Such a contraption might commonly cruise elsewhere, but not in this Eastern Tennessee valley. Its size and satellite dishes captured many eyes on Main Street, but the name splashed on its side caught everyone's attention: Tom Pete and his Bandoliers.

I paid Dinah for my coffee. She followed me out to the street, wiping her hands on a dishtowel.

The driver pulled up to the diesel pumps at the Fuel Farm Truck Stop, and a man stepped down.

"You ain't Tommy Peters," said the attendant accusingly.

"I'm only a roadie. The boss, he's coming."

Gawkers peeked inside. The forty-four-foot Bama-Boy came loaded with full kitchen, entertainment center, and a master suite decorated in—quoting Pastor Ansgar—Early French Prostitute. It packed enough amps, instruments, and audio electronics to broadcast the Grand Ole Opry. And a band, all dressed in Nudie suits—that's Nuta Kotlyarenko, of course, who turned rhinestone cowboys into sparkling country stars.

I fetched my camera from the KLOO news van.

Amid the excitement, up rolled Tommy himself, our local-boy-made-good, driving a brand-new 1978 Corvette in Indy-Pace-Car silver, a car the locals dreamt about but could never hope to afford.

Friends and fans gathered around, shook hands, clapped Tommy on the back, asked about life in Nashville, on the other side of the world. Asked if he missed Suwannechee.

A schoolgirl too young to know his name said, "You a singer?"

"That I am."

"How come you ain't singing us something?"

Tom chuckled with pleasure. From the passenger seat, he retrieved a Martin acoustic.

My annoyance and occasional friend Ray Kaye sidled up to me.

"Reckon he stopped 'side the road, unwrapped his guitar like he done for Holly Ansgar ten years ago. Betcha he tuned it and brushed that Tom Petty hair before his royal entrance."

"Ray, I'm not recording your damn gossip. Stop that crap."

Resting a hip on the Vette's fender, Tommy plucked strings and pretended to adjust pegs. Choreographed one by one, the Bandoliers stepped down from the RV, instruments in hand. On their leader's nod, they launched into "Ramblin' Gamblin' Floyd."

The band posed before the hubcap-studded feed store. For the next twenty-five minutes, my Nikon snapped Tommy singing to that little girl, Tommy tipping a slouch hat over one eye, Tommy being group-hugged by our Daisy Maes in their Daisy Dukes.

Strumming guitars and banjos, the Bandoliers strolled like troubadours to the tooth-gap park where consolidation had demolished the schoolhouse. At the gazebo steps, they segued into love ballads.

Those getting off work stopped to listen. Corndog, the village pooch, thumped his tail. Couples old and young embraced, undulating to bluegrass 'n' blues.

Chords strummed as Tom leaned into the crowd. "Maybe you heard of a friend of mine. He wrote a sweet song called 'Turnabout,' 'bout a Southern boy and a proactive girl taking a second chance."

More felt than heard, melancholy notes trembled in the air. Callused, work-hardened fingers, household-reddened and raw from endless rubbing, scrubbing, and garden grubbing, enclosed petite hands. Villagers danced. Women nestled against chests, lashes brushing whiskers. Magnolia pollen dampened men's eyes. Lips found lips. Lovers swayed.

The whoop of a siren jarred the mood, as a Ford Interceptor nosed through the crowd and stopped at the gazebo, bringing the impromptu concert to a standstill. A pudgy figure hefted its way out of the cruiser.

Tommy grinned. "Well, well, if it ain't our hall monitor. How ya doing, Riley?"

Sheriff Bulwark hadn't yet succumbed to the fat-Southern-deputy stereotype, but he'd been studying the brochure. Hooking thumbs in his service belt, he ignored Tommy's outstretched hand.

"What you doing here, Peters? You lost?"

"Whoa, the local law doesn't like me. Why is that, Riley? Most counties, the sheriff serves the people, but here in Suwannechee—"

"I axed you a question, Peters. Why're you here? You ain't welcome."

"A man's entitled to go where he wants, when he wants."

"Peters, you step out of line, I'll nail your ass. I shoulda *kicked* it long ago."

"My, my. All this hostility and me here to help the town."

"How could you possibly help us?"

Tom grinned. He plucked five notes on his guitar: two six-teenths, two eighths, and a half.

The crowd hushed, then cheered. Strummer Frankie Riser echoed the riff, the signature bars of "Dueling Banjos."

Peters turned to the crowd. "Been thinking about the situation here in my hometown. No McDonald's, no mall or factory, no money, no hope. Other places got underwater mortgages. Washington leaves *us* underwater houses. Come 1979, bring a snorkel."

"Tell 'em, Tommy."

"Remember my song 'Harper Valley TVA'? Lawyers climbed on my ass faster than Sheriff Bulwark sniffing out a church picnic. Nashville attorneys say I can't borrow Tom T. Hall's tune, and Washington legal fellers complain I slandered the tender feelings of the Tennessee Valley Authority. What's a country boy to do when the government floods his hometown?"

"Hell with 'em!"

"Amen. We're gonna throw ourselves a fundraiser. Call it Flood Aid, a last hurrah concert for the good folks in the Su-wannechee Valley. You'll see all your favorite Opry stars plus a new guy, John Mellencamp—don't call him Johnny Cougar—coming down all the way from Indiana. You decide. Do we stage a concert to help our neighbors?"

At the periphery hovered a young woman. Her all-growed-up appearance belied a Delta Dawn fragility that tugged masculine heartstrings. The day Tommy Peters left town, Holly Ansgar wept on the bank of the Suwannechee. Now, tears streamed down her cheeks, much as they had then.

Riley Bulwark backed his cruiser from the park and swung by the lady. He leaned over and threw his passenger door half open. After ten seconds, he tapped his horn. "Holly, get your ass in the car."

Either his ex-wife didn't see him or couldn't hear above the music. He peeled away, fragging her shins with gravel, his door swinging shut.

Tom clapped my shoulder.

"Great to see you, Walt. I heard KLOO hired you. That your van?"

"Station's van, not mine."

"Roberta still studio manager? Never seen a news truck without giant call letters splashed on it."

"We're known for stealth reporting."

Tom laughed. "Roberta's still too cheap to pay for a professional paint job?"

"Bingo in one," I said. "We're lighting a bonfire tonight. Want to join us?"

"Thanks, my friend, but after driving from Duluth, I'm exhausted. I need some shuteye."

As Tommy crossed the street to the Nestle Inn, Ray Kaye arrived with a pickup bed of split wood and bourbon. Ray said, "Boys, not long now, where you're sittin's gonna sink like Atlantis. Let's build us one last bonfire."

Sheltered in the lee of the armory, flames flared heavenward. Camaraderie wafted on wood smoke.

Tom's plan intrigued folks. They would shake a last defiant fist in the face of the universe while gathering a little money for those in need. And everyone here was in need.

The village looked to Roger Mulls, the last-but-one senior class president before consolidation, as their leader.

"Roger, what you think?"

"Lord knows this town's due a break and a boost. To pull this off, we need a venue to host thousands of visitors. Large place, like a pasture. I'm thinking Schrier Fields, been abandoned two, three years. The cliff walls make an acoustical shell, a natural amphitheater."

Late-nighters talked 'til three. Lots of folks didn't make it to church in the morning. But Tom Peters did.

Azariah Vikarsen St. Ansgar reminded me of Ichabod Crane. He favored a Guy Fawkes 'stache 'n' beard beneath a crow's beak that sniffed rarified air. The Reverend Doctor might have startled the Addams family, but Vic Ansgar knew how to preach.

His Holy Gospel One-in-Jesus-Christ Interdenominational Church of Our Savior contracted with KLOO, 1070 on the radio dial and channel thirty-four on UHF TV, to deliver the Word of God and roast His adversaries over fire and brimstone.

On occasion, the Lord took matters into His own hands and interrupted the broadcast signal. Like the rest of the soon-to-be-abandoned infrastructure, valley transmission lines received minimal maintenance. KLOO suffered outages whenever a sparrow perched on a utility pole.

I was usually on call on Sundays—and Reverend Ansgar always called.

"Brother Walter, today's sermon addresses a seminal crisis. If those TV lines go down, I'll ride your ass into Jerusalem."

Vic Ansgar graduated a year ahead of us, his sister Holly a year behind. A child of tent-revivalist parents who mercilessly beat him, he deserved our pity, my mother said.

His parents burned to death in a horrific trailer fire. Arson, the authorities concluded. Mom said, "What else could go wrong for that poor boy?"

He rebounded, developed a Svengali ability to mesmerize crowds. Career advisers recommended law school, but he returned to his roots: firebrand religion.

When Pastor Ansgar preached hellfire gospel, the placid 1798 Southern Methodist Church couldn't compete. That left Bridgewater Baptist across the river vying for souls with the Hole-in-One, as wags called the Holy One-in-Jesus Church, though never in Ansgar's presence.

Tom parked his Vette in the churchyard near my van. Considering their history, I hadn't expected him to attend Rev Ansgar's little chats about death and damnation. Inside the church, eyebrows raised, but Ray Kaye scooted over his family to make room.

Tom nodded to parishioners.

Reverend Ansgar scowled at the interruption.

Glances slid in the direction of Holly Ansgar, who stared rigidly straight ahead.

Tom leaned toward me. "Ever think our minister's Vandyke looks more Satanic than saintly? Like Abe Lincoln's evil brother?"

"His gift is his larynx," I whispered. "Gland of silk and money."

Ansgar glowered. He bellowed: "Thus the younger son layeth naked with harlots and whores. He gambled and committed the most debauched and depraved sins. But unlike you who transgress, the day came that he realized his mistakes. He returned to his father. Liberal churches won't explain that punishment comes before salvation. In gospel too dangerous to teach, the father bullwhips his prodigal boy within an inch of his life. He lashes and scourges the sinning son"—the pastor paused to dab his cheeks—"until the blood of redemption runneth in rivulets down his back. Remember henceforth this Word."

He glared around the chapel.

"Strangers come slithering amongst us. Philanders and fornicators ravish and rape our women, our wives, our daughters and sisters." He swelled in outrage. "They rendereth tramps, trollops, trulls, and whores, degenerate *débauchées*. A righteous Lord striketh—"

Holly Ansgar shot to her feet and stalked out of the sanctuary.

Ignoring knowing looks, Tom Peters rose and followed. I trailed after them.

Tom caught up with her and reached for her sleeve. "Holly." His voice wavered.

She spun. "You, you *bastard*. You abandoned me."

Her small fists pounded Peters's chest. Standing with open palms, he endured the assault. She teetered in her heels. Tom whispered. Whatever he said, she wilted. She collapsed against him.

"I felt so hurt," Holly sobbed, "so confused. I said yes to

Riley because I hated myself more than I hated you."

Time melted. Tom nuzzled her hair, his lips met hers.

He was still holding her when the sheriff's cruiser skidded to a stop.

"Peters, let go of my wife."

"Wife? I thought you two were divorced."

"Riley," said Holly. "Leave us, please. I have a lot to atone for."

"The hell I will. Hands behind you, Peters. Now."

I stepped forward. "You'll bogus arrest him on camera?"

Bulwark spun toward me.

"Damn you, Walt. Butt out of my private business. Get back in the church."

"Not happening, Riley. Arrests are public interest."

"I'll jail you both."

"At least I'll see Peters gets there intact."

Bulwark reddened. "What's that supposed to mean?"

"Everyone's heard talk how Sheriff Wade died."

"All right, Peters. Go. Run fast. Your day will come."

Riley's predecessor, Sheriff Burl Wade, had arrived a Yankee, but he had quickly embraced Southern sensibilities. Scrupulously fair, reluctant to over-react, he erred on the side of compassion. He never angered, not until the day little Jenny Aiken died.

Public facts remained few: an obscenely wealthy dynasty, the Aikens, early settlers, former slave owners. One rebellious grand-child. One Reverend Ansgar, casting out demons. Flagellations. Death.

The tight-lipped sheriff would not, as the family later put it, listen to reason. He booked Ansgar and the Aikens into jail.

Late that night, Sheriff Wade's Jeep inexplicably plunged off Outlook Mountain Road.

Rookie Riley Bulwark declared it an accident and rushed Wade's body to Gatlin Mortuary instead of the coroner. Acting on his own, Riley cleared the scene before calling consternated THP investigators.

Devoid of evidence incinerated in the crash, the suspects were released with apologies. In the ensuing special election, Aikens and Ansgar threw their support behind twenty-year-old Riley, electing him the youngest sheriff in Tennessee history.

Concert fever caught fire. As weeks dropped from the calendar, residents unstintingly pitched in to help promoters, producers, and their experts in logistics, victuals, money handling, medical staffing, crowd control, and waste disposal.

One month from showtime, Tom sought me out. "Have you seen Holly?"

"Sorry, Tom. Can't think the last time I saw her."

"Let me know if you hear anything."

She didn't show at church on Sunday. After setting up the transmitters, I threaded back roads to the reverend's country estate, home of Tennessee Walkers and Kentucky thoroughbreds. Televangelism had blest Reverend Ansgar.

In the stable yard, I found no one, nary a groom nor stable hand, not even a horse. Ansgar's antediluvian evacuation would've pleased Noah proud.

An arbor path led to the pastor's antebellum McMansion. I rapped on the service entrance. Nothing. I rounded a wing to the front.

The sheriff spotted me before I noticed him, yipped his siren, gunned his engine, and skidded to a halt beside me.

"What're you doing here, Wally? Why ain't you attending services?"

"Miss Ansgar is absent today. I wondered if she needed any-thing. Why're *you* here?"

"Vic received some death threats, so I'm keeping an eye on the house."

"I haven't heard anything about death threats."

"You wouldn't, would you? Better get back to church. I'll escort you to your truck, so you don't get lost."

Riley watched as I climbed aboard my van. He didn't bother nodding as I pulled out, retracing country roads toward town.

"He's not following, is he?" came a voice from behind me.

"Jesus." My heart leaped against my ribcage. "Holly? What are you doing here?"

"Running."

"From what?"

Her fear-laced sweat reached my nostrils.

"They locked me up, Riley and my brother."

"Why?"

"They think Riley owns me."

"What am I supposed to do with you? I can't hide you four weeks until the concert."

"I don't want to hide. Get me a room at the hotel, right up front, first floor. With everyone watching, I'll be safe."

I dropped her at the Nestle Inn. It was broad daylight on a Sunday morning, but I couldn't help glancing over my shoulder.

Tom and Holly couldn't stay apart. Breakfasting at Dinah's Diner, I told him, "You look haggard as hell, pal."

"While she sleeps, I stay awake. Holly can't relax unless I keep watch."

"You got perseverance. Fourteen more days, and everything comes together. Your people have built quite a village in Schrier Fields."

"A gypsy camp, like a circus. When done, we'll fold our tents and trailers and depart into the ether."

"Rumor says Loomis Armored can't cross McAllister Bridge to pick up the gate receipts."

"Probably true," Tom said. "Our motorhome barely made it over that rickety scrap iron. An armored truck weighs tons more. Filled with men, fuel, and money, it way exceeds the bridge limit."

"For a two-hundred-K fee, Bridgewater Borough proposed ticket booths on their side of the river. Promoters turned them down. They accepted Riley's recommendation, a plain commercial van."

"Bulwark thought that up?"

"That money means a lot to people here," I said. "It'll help them start new lives. What about you, Tom? Back to Nashville?"

"I'll go as far away as possible. Them kidnapping Holly made it clear we'll never be safe here. We need to get out of Tennessee, maybe the country. She's applied for a passport."

"That drastic? You think they'd come after you?"

"Hell, yes, says the creepy feeling in my spine."

Understanding the players, I reluctantly agreed.

"Riley's amazing investigative skills have deduced she still loves me," Tom said. "You know, he abused her psychologically. 'No man wants a slut like you,' like that. Her goddamn brother administered scourges."

"I had no idea."

"That Sunday in the churchyard, if you hadn't stepped in, you'd've never seen me alive again."

KLOO's broadcast licenses facilitated streaming the concert live. Once our satellite dishes locked on-line, our sleepy operation became the Little Station That Could.

The first campers arrived early Thursday. By evening, the trickle had become a flow. Vendors erected craft and T-shirt booths. Smoked ribs and fried onions scented the air. Brandishing a microphone, I wandered among the attendees, seeking personal-interest stories.

Friday unveiled a day of perfect weather. Hard Knox, the first in a series of regional bands, opened the show. Reba McEntire took the stage as the evening's headliner.

Rolling Stone gifted me a press pass, in case security questioned KLOO's plain white van. I shuttled correspondents from a dozen countries. I hadn't expected such enthusiastic foreigners.

Friday passed as a blur, Saturday much the same. Booze kept the medical and security staffs busy.

"The Kendalls," I told everyone in the mess tent. "I'm going radio silent tonight to catch their act. Don't call me unless Miss Jeannie requires mouth-to-mouth resuscitation."

At eight-forty p.m., I grabbed a lawn chair. I sauntered out the backstage gate, turning away pleas to let way-too-young ladies through the portal. That kind of trouble, no guy needs.

The show? Wow! Jeannie Kendall? *Wrrrrow!* After their performance, still humming "Heaven's Just a Sin Away," I dragged my chair backstage and headed for the car park.

What the hell? I'm a considerate park-between-the-lines guy, but damn, my van now sprawled across three spaces chalked in the grass.

When I stuck my key in the ignition, it jammed. What now? My Bic showed the ignition had been ripped apart. On the floor lay a glove and a foot-long screwdriver.

Security acted more puzzled than helpful.

"Your vehicle's been moved fifteen feet? Someone's screwing with you, man—but we got a more serious prob at the moment."

"Like what?"

"We ain't supposed to talk about it. I might not have a job tomorrow." He glanced over his shoulder. "We've been hit."

"Hit?"

"Robbed. Hour ago, a van backed up to cash control, flashed papers. We loaded Friday's and Saturday's receipts, and off it went."

"Today's *and* yesterday's? How come?"

"Yesterday, no truck showed up. My boss called Wells Fargo. They told him someone canceled the pickup. You can imagine the shitstorm."

My reporter's nose twitched. "So double the receipts were on hand today?"

"Yeah. This plain white van backed in, not an armored truck, just like we were told to expect. We loaded it, and good riddance. After Friday's fallout, we were eager to pack it the hell out of here. Thirty minutes later, another van showed up. We figured Wells Fargo accidentally sent two trucks, but no. The money vanished into the night. We're suspects now, the whole lot of us."

Sheriff Bulwark stomped into the tent and strode directly to me. "You got guts, Wally. Spill—and spare me the crap, understand?"

I tried to stand up, but he shoved me back in the folding chair. I couldn't see his face without craning my neck.

"What?" I said. "Somebody screwed with my van. I'm reporting it."

Riley pressed uncomfortably near. His uniform smelled like a Fryolator. "Real common car thief trick," he said, "hammering a screwdriver into the lock. A dumbass reporter mighta done it to fool us."

"Riley, I came in here to report a problem, not get pushed around."

"Sheriff Bulwark to you, gutterballs. Your plain white truck's identical to the Wells Fargo van. You and your buds think I wouldn't notice?"

Riley up close was not a thing of beauty with his lint pills and sweat stains, an undone pouch fastener on his service belt. I wanted to snap it closed, but he'd probably arrest me for assault.

"Sheriff, I discovered the damage to my van after the Kendalls's concert. Period, full stop."

"Bullshit. Where's Peters's RV?"

"What?"

"Our boy's run off in his motorhome. Want to tell me where he's hiding? Or did your buddy abandon you? Scoot off with your share of the loot?"

"Riley, you're an idiot. Last I saw, Tommy was chatting with Randy Travis."

"He's fled over the river and through the woods. Don't go nowhere."

He hitched up his trousers and turned away. His holster-in-your-face diplomacy chilled me to the core.

Holly Ansgar, it turned out, was also gone. The Nestle Inn clerk told me a single phone call had come in, and she'd packed a bag and walked out the door. Arriving guests prevented him from noticing who picked her up.

On-air, Sheriff Bulwark announced the disappearance of the weekend's cash proceeds, roughly calculated at one-point-three million. In retrospect, his antipathy toward Tommy seemed amply justified.

"Folks, Tom Peters robbed from the poor and gave to his own self-enrichment. He denied Valley residents a chance to make their hard lives easier. Tom, if you're listening, turn yourself in before us good ol' boys find you."

In lieu of levity and laughter, the roadies packed up in silence. Attendees trudged home from the campgrounds. Tom's bandmates complained angrily about their missing gear and motorhome in a *Mother Jones* interview.

The RV had simply disappeared. Most figured it would turn up in Chattanooga, Charlottesville, Chicago, or Chihuahua, repainted and repurposed.

A report clacked over the telex from Knoxville. Two airline tickets had been purchased in the name of Thomas Peters, destination El Paso, across the border from Ciudad Juárez. Texas Rangers met the plane when it touched down, but Tom and Holly were not aboard.

After the ill-fated concert, the tabloids picked apart the players. Quoting *Us Weekly*, Ansgar's sister Holly never again was seen in public. Those who claimed to know said Holly had joined Tom Pete on the run, fleeing her ex-husband and overbearing brother.

The dam garroted the throat of the Suwannechee River. Over the years, locals fished the man-made lake, boated, skied, and snorkeled. Scuba divers explored the ancient Methodist Church perched on its underwater hill.

The Hole-in-One exploded into a mega-church, a ministerial money magnet. The Reverend Vikarsen St. Ansgar spread the gospel in a private Gulfstream. More than a million a week poured in for the tough-talking televangelist.

Riley Bulwark abandoned law enforcement but not law-and-order. Attired in a thousand-dollar suit, he rode his platform into the Tennessee State Legislature. Six years later, three-thousand-dollar suits and a superbly funded campaign elevated him to Congress.

2003

As the concert's twenty-fifth anniversary loomed, the TVA and Bureau of Reclamation jointly announced they would drain the reservoir for dam maintenance and repair. Scientists, historians, and news outlets took notice.

Congressman Bulwark seemed the obvious choice to oversee the lowering of his district's lake, but he initially demurred. His press secretary announced, "Duties in Washington preclude his pulling that ol' bathtub plug." Critical editorials changed his mind.

Most of the press treated the draining of the dam with indifference, but not *Rolling Stone*. Its editors asked me to compose a retrospective. I hesitated, but I had something to say, words that had simmered for a quarter century.

After the Army Corp of Engineers gave the nod, I drove across the rickety bridge to the old Fuel Farm Truck Stop, once at the edge of town. There, the Bureau of Reclamation headquartered their command vehicles on the embankment. Before joining them, I glanced around.

The diseased remains of the dead village frightened and fascinated me. Rotting algae had softened and rounded sharp edges. Weeds hungry for real estate were reclaiming the soil of their ancestors. The old armory walls still stood, bricks coated with gelatinous slime. Farther down the reservoir's slope, a malodorous fecal-grey glop covered a Lovecraftian landscape.

To assist, the local RC hobbyist club stepped in. With cameras on quadcopters, drones zoomed like insects, figuring out coordinates in a land never mapped by GPS, cataloguing elevations, rail lines and fragments of roads. Few landmarks and an unrecognizable terrain made figuring boundaries and points of interest slow going.

The stink of decayed vegetation cloyed my nostrils. I was pouring a paper cup of coffee when a drone operator said, "What's that?"

The camera image showed a mud-covered vehicle stranded in the middle of nowhere.

"Where *is* that?" I asked.

"According to the county plat maps, that land belonged to A.V. St. Ansgar."

"Ansgar's McMansion." Recalling the day Holly had hidden in my van, I traced a finger to an adjacent foundation. "Call the sheriff," I said.

Brian Douglass was the antithesis of former Sheriff Bulwark—not pudgy, not sloppy, not bullying, not white. He listened carefully to what I had to say.

He said, "You don't tell me what or why, but you think I need to visit that bus?"

"It's not a bus. It's a motorhome in a now-collapsed barn."

"And?"

"An RV disappeared in the wake of Tom Peters."

"Yeah, I heard of him, long gone with the money."

"Sheriff, with or without you, I'm taking a helicopter out

there. I thought it might interest you and save me hiring my own transport."

"Hold on, old son. I didn't say I wasn't interested. My can-openers need tools, gloves, boots, and God knows what. You think that old rust bucket might offer a clue where the money went?"

"Maybe," I said, without conviction.

County One lifted out of Bridgewater and followed coordinates to the Ansgar plantation. The chopper hovered, then landed on a relatively clear spot, once the cement floor of stables.

The stench of dying fish trapped in pools assaulted our senses. We slipped and slid on the slimy concrete.

Police Explorers from the Boy Scouts shoveled mud to clear a path. The vehicle revealed itself, clearly an RV, not a bus. Its tires had rotted on the starboard side but not on the left, and it canted eerily.

"Boys, thanks. Take a break, fellows."

Exacerbated by the tilt, the cab door hung open.

"Flashlights," Douglass ordered, and the Explorers slapped electric lanterns in our hands.

"This thing's cavernous," the sheriff said. "Passenger sofas…a rotted guitar…piles of vintage CDs, wow. Mammoth console…driver's seat and…*whoa*." His voice faltered. "Oh, shit. Oh, my God."

"Easy, man," I said. "I tried to warn you."

Douglass swallowed, staring everywhere but at the two skeletons entwined in the seat. "Oh, Jesus, man. Corpses I can handle. But fucking handcuffs through the steering wheel? Christ, nightmares will haunt me for ages."

As we lifted off, the sheriff's dispatch called.

The sheriff listened intently, then spoke into the mic: "Not until I get there. Have a car meet me at the airport. See the Scouts get home."

He disconnected and handed me a Kevlar vest. Before we landed, another dispatch came in.

"Sheriff, Beech N341P filed a flight plan to Bridgewater Municipal. It fell off the radar at Clingmans Dome. You know who we mean, right?"

"Jesus, God," Douglass said. "The Reverend's last amen."

"Took the words right out of my mouth."

A Boy Scout with a Boston accent said, "Clingmans Dome?"

His buddy replied before I thought of a gentler answer: "Tallest peak in the Great Smokies."

As we drove, evening's curtain descended. Douglass delegated duties in rapid fire. By the time his driver crept up to the McAllister Bridge, Washington had the NTSB on their way to the mountains.

"Stay back," the sheriff told me. He turned to the figure leaning against the railing of the old iron structure. "Congressman, you mind if I call you Riley? What can I do for you?"

Bulwark lit a cigar. The flare of the match revealed a snubnose revolver in his hand. He took a drag and said, "In my day, law and order took precedence. Someone got civil disruptive, me and the boys took 'em for a little education behind the barn."

"You're condoning a double murder?" Douglass bowed his head. "A quarter century Peters has cradled her in his lap, handcuffed to the goddamn steering wheel."

"Listen here, Sheriff. Vic was the brains, I was the brawn. We made a good team. Except not *that* evening. Vic told me to hand him my Colt and cuffs and skedaddle. Only later he told me he'd left them tombed to drown."

"His own sister."

"He might preach Jesus, but Vic's strictly Old Testament. He cast out the harlot. I reckon Wally over there guessed. That right, Sherlock? You knew?"

Disgust churned my gut. "In the tent," I said, "your gun belt.

24

The utility pouch for your handcuffs was empty. After Tommy's near-arrest at church, I kept associating missing cuffs with missing persons."

"Hmmph." Riley flicked ash from his cigar.

I said, "Performers wouldn't know squat about the cash pickup; Tommy spent his free time at Holly's hotel. But law enforcement knew. You recommended a plain, nondescript van. You knew how to cancel Friday's pickup."

"That don't prove nothing."

"Sadly, the State Police agreed. Suspicions weren't evidence. I believed you'd never get caught."

"Wouldn't have, if some dumbass engineer hadn't found failing sluices, spillways, whatever. We figured we'd be long dead and gone by the time that RV came to light."

The sheriff said, "Riley, let's wrap this."

"You got a smooth way about you, Douglass. But here's what's gonna happen. Vic Ansgar and I been planning this for twenty-five years. He's picking me up in his fancy aeroplane, and we're gonna fly to one of them rum-and-margarita islands."

"You talk with Ansgar recently?"

"Called him soon as y'all found the bodies. He should get here any minute now."

"Don't think so. Your warning changed his plans."

"How's that?"

"Ansgar swan-dived into the Great Smokies."

"No, that ain't so." The congressman's cigar twitched. He turned toward me. "Walt, don't lie to me. What he's saying's true?"

I nodded. "As we landed, it came in on the radio."

"Bastard." Bulwark gripped his pistol. "You saying there's no way out?"

"Put the gun down, Riley."

"Bullshit. I took out my first sheriff when you was wetting nappies, Douglass. I'm gonna off all y'all, starting with Wally there."

Douglass stepped in front of me.

"Riley, Riley. You see my deputies, there, there, and there? You're looking at the finest squirrel hunters in the state. Penny behind the truck-stop ruins? She can thread a .22 through a migrating goose's eye. She'll snuff the ash from your stogie without ruffling your eyelash. And my other boys got *better* aim."

Riley instinctively raised his cigar.

Three shots rang out.

The slugs took out his kneecaps. Bulwark collapsed over his dropped revolver.

"Sorry, old man," Douglass said. "I tried to tell you. We don't play suicide by cop."

But Riley, hunched on damaged knees, scrabbled for his pistol. He jammed the stubby muzzle under his jaw and pulled the trigger.

While red and blue lights flashed, EMTs worked on Bulwark. After ten minutes, a paramedic pulled off his latex gloves and approached Sheriff Douglass.

"The bastard took out his left jawbone and blew out his ear canal. He'll live, but he'll be eating baby mash through a tube 'til his rotten heart gives out."

Doomed romance touches the heart. Once the Bonnie and Clyde meme collapsed, global news correspondents flew in. That ignited the salvation: the rehabilitation of Tom Pete's reputation. French, Italian, and British reporters compared the tragedy to Abélard et Héloïse, Paolo e Francesca, Lancelot and Guinevere.

The Bandoliers's "The Legend of Tom and Holly" charted three weeks at number one. EMI remastered Tommy's Grammy-nominated album, *Angry Woods and Swirling Waters*. Bob Geldof assembled a pantheon of musicians to sing a eulogy.

For the funeral at Lake Suwannechee, the State of Tennessee donated a double coffin. During the candlelight vigil, the lines mooring the casket inexplicably severed. Before the officials could react, it floated off, disappearing into the sunset.

Today, waters again lap the Suwannechee's shores.
Fish swim. Birds warble.
Salvation sings. Peace reigns.
The locals say God has returned.
Far, far below, sunlight dapples an aquatic hollow. In that bower lie Tom Peters and Holly Ansgar, forever hand in hand.

A White Sport Coat and a Pink Crustacean
Released 1973

"The Great Filling Station Holdup"
"Railroad Lady"
"He Went to Paris"
"Grapefruit—Juicy Fruit"
"Cuban Crime of Passion"
"Why Don't We Get Drunk (and Screw)"
"Peanut Butter Conspiracy"
"They Don't Dance Like Carmen No More"
"I Have Found Me a Home"
"My Lovely Lady"
"Death of an Unpopular Poet"

All songs by Jimmy Buffett,
except "Railroad Lady" (with Jerry Jeff Walker)
and "Cuban Crime of Passion" (with Tom Corcoran).

THE GREAT FILLING STATION HOLDUP

Josh Pachter

"...trust your car to the man who wears the star," Helmut Erhard hummed, filling his beat-up K5 Blazer's tank with regular at the Te-Jo's on the corner of East Brown and Norwood, "the big, bright Texaco star!"

He remembered when the Te-Jo's *was* a Texaco station, back when he was a kid. His daddy used to take him along on Sunday afternoons in his 1962 aquamarine Ford Galaxie Starliner, give him a shiny Roosevelt dime for an ice-cold Co-Cola from the blocky red cooler outside the office while the man who wore the star pumped Sky Chief for thirty-one cents a gallon and checked the oil and squeegeed the windows for free, all part of the service.

Erhard missed those days. By 2001, when the Texas Company merged with Chevron and the big, bright Texaco star began to disappear from gas stations in all but sixteen southern states, his daddy had been gone for sixteen years, dead of a heart attack at fifty-three. There was still a Texaco station down in Bryan, but that was twenty miles south on Highway 190, and forty miles there and back was a long way to go for nostalgia's sake.

"Got a minute?" Frank Bodine, the leathery old codger who owned the Te-Jo's, called from his perch on a wooden stool by the front door. There was an ice machine now where the cooler used to be, and nestled up beside it Frank was likely a sight more

31

comfortable than he'd be inside the office on a hot, dry July afternoon in Hearne, smack-dab in the middle of the triangle formed by Dallas, Houston, and San Antone.

Racking the pump handle, Erhard strolled over. "Used to be a Co-Cola machine right there where you're sitting," he said.

"Every damn time you stop by here," Bodine grumbled, struggling to his feet, "you say the same damn thing." He went into the office and came out with two dewy cans of Coke. "You need to get you some new material, Helmut," he said, handing one over.

"Aaah," Erhard sighed, pressing the cold can to his forehead. "That feels nice."

"Tastes good, too," Bodine said, settling back onto his stool, "you pop it open and have yourself a swaller."

"Frank," Erhard said, following the old man's instructions to the letter, "you are correct, sir. How you been keepin'?"

"I gotta say, Helmut, I been better. You ain't heard I got stuck up?"

Leaning against the closed office door, Erhard narrowed his eyes and resettled his orange Longhorns ball cap. "Stuck up? When?"

"Last Friday night, 'bout eleven p.m., just as I was fixin' to lock the pumps and head for home."

"I had *not* heard. You call it in?"

"Natchally I called it in. But I swear, that new sheriff they hired after Mitch got convicted's 'bout as useful as a drum with a hole in it. He ain't done nothin' but tell me they's workin' on it. That's why I waved you over. I want to hire you to look into the matter, private-like."

"Gotta say, Frank, I don't know I can do much the cops ain't already doin'."

"Sure, I know that. But I'm out six hundred dollars, a can of STP, and a big ol' jar of cashew nuts. I don't mind handin' you another couple hundred, if they's a chance I'll get back what those kids stole."

"Two hundred dollars'd buy anybody else four hours of my time," Erhard said. "I reckon I owe you something for this here Co-Cola, though. How 'bout I put two days' work into your situation and see what I can come up with?"

A frown flickered across Bodine's weathered face. "I ain't askin' for no charity, son. I can afford two hundred bucks. You think you can get anywhere in only four hours, though?"

"This ain't got nothin' to do with charity, Frank," Erhard said, "any more than you givin' me a cold Coke on a hot day. This is just the way you do for a friend. So whyn't you just shut your pie hole and say thanks?"

"I," the old man began. But then he stopped himself and wiped the back of his hand across his mouth. "Thanks," he said. "Thank you kindly, my friend."

Over the next ten minutes, Frank Bodine told Erhard everything he knew about the youngsters who'd robbed him, which wasn't much. There'd been two of them, seemed to be teenagers, dressed identically in dusty jeans and chambray shirts and work boots, each with a knitted ski mask pulled over his head to disguise his face and hair. One of them had yanked a pistol from his pocket and ordered Frank in an obviously phony voice to empty out the cash register. The other one hadn't said a word.

"Normal for you to have six hundred dollars in cash in the till?" Erhard asked.

"Hell, no," Bodine snorted, "not on a weeknight, anyways. But this was Friday, payday, I had people in and out all evening stockin' up on groceries. Friday's my busy day. I figure those damn hoodlums either knew that or made themselves a lucky guess."

Once he'd gotten all the information he could get out of Frank Bodine, Erhard headed over to the Hearne Police Department's one-story brick building on West 3rd, across the street from Emmett Aguirre Bail Bonds and Ninfa's Hair Designs. He left the Blazer in one of the diagonal slots out front of the cop shop and went on in.

"Looking for an update on the robbery over at Te-Jo's, Harlan," he told the desk sergeant, Harlan Washington, a jovial African-American he knew from fish fries at the VFW south of town. "Anything you can tell me?"

"Don't have much to tell," Washington admitted, setting down the pack of cards from which he'd been dealing himself hands of blackjack. "We been busy as a one-legged man at an ass-kicking contest 'round here since the new chief came aboard. Sent Ursie out to talk to Frank Bodine, but she didn't get much from him. Perps were kids, he said, wore ski masks, one of 'em had a gun. Took him for five, six hundred dollars."

Ursula Cantrell was the Hearne PD's only female detective. She was a solidly built woman with close-cropped bottle-blond hair, and the scuttlebutt around town was she was probably a lesbian. Erhard couldn't see that her sexual preference made a bit of difference, and he couldn't see it was anybody's business but Ursie's. She was a good cop, that was all he cared about.

"Prob'ly ought to check in with her," he said, "see if there's any new developments. She around?"

"I reckon she's in back," Washington told him, swinging open the hinged partition that separated the narrow lobby area from the rest of the station. "You know the way."

She *was* in back, in the break room, pouring what smelled like pretty good coffee from a glass carafe into a yellow ceramic mug with a picture of the Lorax on it. "Helmut Erhard," she smiled. "Coffee's fresh. Can I interest you in a cup?"

"A cup of coffee sounds pretty good, Urs. I'd be much obliged."

"Sugar? Milk? We don't have no cream."

"Oh, black'll do me just fine. I want cream and sugar, I'll head over to the DQ for a Blizzard."

"No milk, no sugar," the detective said, taking a disposable paper cup from a plastic bag beside the Mr. Coffee and filling it to the brim. "This a social call, Helmut?"

"Guess not," he said. "Frank Bodine over to the Te-Jo's says y'all aren't making much headway on that robbery he had there. He's hired me to see if I can come up with something you might've missed. I figured I'd start here, see what you could tell me."

"Bodine's a little cracked in the head, ain't he?" Cantrell grinned. "He didn't have a lot to give me, Helmut. Two kids in ski masks, one of 'em packing heat, that's about it. You know how many kids we got here in Hearne?" A sly look came over her face. "Say, I been meaning to ask you, you put the Erhard moves on Bonnie Barnes yet? I know you've always had a kind of a thing for her."

You got some ideas in that direction yourself, Ursie? was what he wanted to say, but it really *wasn't* any of his business, so he kept the thought to himself and answered her question.

"Just bidin' my time," he said. "Mitch ain't been locked up but three months. I hear Bonnie's filed for a divorce. I figure I'll leave her be 'till it's final and then, I don't know, maybe. She *is* a good woman, always has been."

"I say go for it, man. You and her, I can totally see that."

"Mitch must've been flat-out crazy," Erhard sighed, "getting himself mixed up with Elsie Jordan. That girl was young enough to be his granddaughter."

"Mitch had us all fooled," the detective said. "I like to *died* when you figured out he was the one who killed her."

"Y'all take care, now," Erhard said, finishing the last of his coffee and tossing the empty cup into the trash. "I'll let y'all know when I crack the great filling-station holdup for you."

Back in his Blazer with the a.c. going full blast, Erhard sat hunched over the wheel, considering what to do next.

Unless the two kids who'd jacked the Te-Jo's started bragging on it or spending the proceeds, he wasn't sure how he was going to pin the crime on any of the town's teens. One of them had a pistol, according to Frank Bodine, but the population of Hearne was more than four thousand, and he wouldn't be a bit surprised if there weren't several hundred handguns inside the city limits, given the state's absence of background checks for firearms purchases and the open-carry legislation Governor Greg Abbott signed into law in 2015.

Finally thinking *Kids*, he backed out of his parking space and retraced his way to Brown. Instead of turning left toward Frank Bodine's place of business, though, he turned right and drove seven-tenths of a mile southwest past the Oxtail Factory and Becky's Mexican toward Hearne High School. *If you're looking for a pair of needles*, he thought, *you mize well head straight for the haystack.*

For almost a year now, Erhard and HHS principal Tito Rodriguez had been meeting up every other Saturday night for a beer—sometimes, truth be told, a couple beers—at the Broken Stool, a working-class bar in a little strip mall on West Brown, sandwiched halfway between the car wash and the Regis Taqueria. They had met during Erhard's investigation of the Elsie Jordan murder, had sat side by side through most of Mitch Barnes's trial. By the time the jury brought in its guilty verdict after less than an hour of deliberation, they realized that they'd become friends, though the PI was a decade Rodriguez's senior.

Erhard had visited the high school several times since the trial, most recently to do an active-shooter talk in the auditorium, so he knew his way around the building. He found the principal in his office, Charlie Parker's "Anthropology" swinging from the speakers positioned for maximum effect in the corners of the room. As he stepped through the doorway, Miles Davis was just soaring into his solo, Max Roach laying down a syncopated beat in the background.

Tito Rodriguez believed in dressing for success, but it was warm despite the air-conditioning and he had his pinstriped gray suit coat draped over the back of his desk chair, the top button of his white shirt undone and his red power tie loosened.

The fringe of salt-and-pepper hair that ringed his otherwise bald light-brown scalp was damp with perspiration. He was hunched over a thick computer printout, scratching notes in the margins with a fountain pen.

"Am I interrupting?" asked Erhard.

"Nah," Rodriguez said, dropping the pen on the pile of papers and rolling his head back to clear the tension from his neck. "I'm just going over next year's budget. The state's cut us back *again*, and I'm trying to figure out how to keep this place up and running without letting anybody go."

"Don't you get the summer off?"

"A consummation devoutly to be wished," the principal sighed. Erhard figured that was probably either Shakespeare or the Bible. "Most of the faculty do, 'cept the lucky ones teaching summer school for extra pay—which I may not be able to afford a year from now. What's on your mind, Helmut? Something I can do for you?"

"Lookin' into the stick-up over at the Te-Jo's last weekend," Erhard said, dropping into one of the red-vinyl-covered visitors' chairs. "Ol' Frank Bodine says it was 'kids' ripped him off, so I figured—"

"—so you figured you'd go where the kids are," Rodriguez cut in. "That makes sense, *amigo*."

"Only problem," Erhard realized, "is the *kids* have the summer off, too, so you haven't seen them in a month or more."

Tito Rodriguez pursed his lips. "Most of 'em," he said. "We got some of 'em taking summer classes, though, and, now you mention it, there's a boy who's usually pretty well behaved who's been sent to see me twice already this week for acting up in class. I wonder..."

He swiveled to face his computer. His fingers danced across the keyboard, and then he turned back to his friend. "Isaac Flowers," he said. "He's in remedial English right now, gets out in"—he glanced at his watch—"about twenty minutes. I can give the two of you a chem lab we're not using today, if you want to talk to him."

Erhard nodded, as Charlie Parker was replaced on the sound system by Ella Fitzgerald, crooning "Oh! Lady Be Good." Her scat vocal on that tune was one of his favorite things in the world, so he leaned back in his chair and put his hands behind his head. "You go on and get back to your budget," he said. "You don't mind if I wait for young Mr. Flowers here, do you?"

The chemistry lab looked like something out of a low-rent film version of *Frankenstein*, with Bunsen burners and glass beakers, and Erlenmeyer flasks and wooden racks of test tubes, and vials of rainbow-colored chemicals littering the black laminate science table. All that was missing was Igor the hunchback and a bucket of body parts.

Helmut Erhard was sitting at the teacher's desk when Rodriguez led in an obviously frightened boy who couldn't have been more than sixteen years old and, without a word, left the two of them alone.

Isaac Flowers was a scrawny thing, maybe five foot seven, hundred and twenty pounds sopping wet. He had dirty blond hair and a sprinkling of zits on both sides of a nose that looked like it had been broken once upon a time and poorly set. He wore tan chinos that needed a wash and an incongruous Hawaiian shirt decorated with flamingos that was two sizes too big for him. Probably a hand-me-down from his dad or an older brother. He looked around the lab like a bear cub surprised in the act of raiding a campground picnic basket.

"Real nice to meet you, Isaac," Erhard said, sticking out a hand. "Your buddies call you Ike?"

"Don't got no buddies," the boy said, pretending a bravado he clearly didn't feel. "But, yeah, sure, e'body calls me Ike."

He perched on the edge of a shop stool the PI had pulled up to the desk for him.

Erhard kept silent, letting the pressure build.

"Look," the boy said at last, "what you want with me?"

"Maybe for starters you can tell me where you were about eleven o'clock last Friday night," Erhard said.

"Uh, Friday? I don't know. I guess I was home in bed." The kid's hands were trembling, and Erhard's built-in lie detector pinged.

"Tell the truth, now, son. You sure you weren't over at the Te-Jo's with one of those buddies you ain't got and a couple a ski masks—and a handgun? You know the gun makes it aggravated robbery. That's a first-degree felony, Ike, could get you up to ninety-nine years in the big house."

Erhard waited. If Tito Rodriguez was correct, this kid had been wrestling with a big secret all week, and it was like to explode out of him any second.

Right on cue, the boy cracked open like an egg.

"*He* was the one with the gun," Ike Flowers burst out, tears welling in his pale-blue eyes. "I thought we was just gonna put a scare into the old man!"

A half hour later, Erhard pulled off Vaughn Lane onto the dirt track that served as the "main street" of the Encino Estates mobile-home park. "Aggie Owned and Operated," the sign outside the office read, and when Erhard asked her for the Waldron residence, the manager took her Marlboro out of her mouth long enough to point through the window at a beat-up 1953 Silver Star camper in the northwest corner.

Rapping sharply on the side of the wide-open screen door, Erhard yelled, "Kevin? Kevin Waldron? You in there, son?"

"Don't have to shout," came a disembodied voice from somewhere within, and then a figure appeared in the doorway.

Shading his eyes with the palm of his hand, the kid looked down at Erhard like the lord of the manor surveying his serfs.

He was barefoot, dressed in frayed denim cutoffs and a faded white T-shirt that read "Texas AF" in big blue letters. He was maybe a year older than Ike Flowers, an inch and a half taller, twenty pounds more beef on him.

"Okay," he said, "you woke me up. What you want?"

Reaching for his wallet, Erhard produced his private investigator's license. You could buy an official-looking PI badge off the internet for twenty dollars, but that seemed a little too cute. Erhard was happy with his Department of Public Safety-issued laminated ID card.

"Think you and I need to have ourselves a talk," he said, and he pushed past the boy into the camper's wood-paneled interior.

"See, Frank," Erhard said, "the boy's got a situation he didn't know how to deal with, and he did what he sees desperate people do all the time on the TV."

They were sitting outside the Te-Jo's late that afternoon: Erhard, Frank Bodine, and Kevin Waldron, each with a cold Dr Pepper, the three of them passing a bag of Buc-ee's Beaver Nuggets back and forth like old friends.

"On June first," Erhard explained, "Kevin's ma got laid off from her job at the Stop N Save, and that means she lost her health insurance. She and Kevin here are living in a mobile home over to Encino Estates, and there's no way she could afford to go on Cobra."

"Real sorry to hear that, son," said Bodine. "Times are tough, and that's a fact."

"You ain't heard the half of it," Erhard frowned. "The woman's got diabetes. She *was* paying twenty-five dollars a month for insulin, but that was gone go up to four hundred and fifty a month without insurance."

Bodine shook his head sadly. "Goddamn drug comp'nies," he spat. "They won't be happy till they've bankrupted the lot of us."

"You got that right," Kevin chimed in. "So what I'm supposed to do, watch my momma *die*?"

"Junior here roped in a friend whose name I ain't gonna

mention," Erhard went on. "When his daddy took off, a year or so back, he left a rusty old handgun behind, and that's what they used to stick you up. Kevin showed it to me: gun wasn't even loaded, and I don't think it would have fired if it *was*. Still, we turn these kids over to the *po*lice, I reckon their little escapade's gone cost them two good years in juvie."

"Okay," said the old man, "I git the pitcher. I don't suppose we need to rope old Ursie in on this, long as I get my six hundred dollars back—plus let's call it another fifteen bucks for the can of STP and them cashews you boys stole."

"See, that's the problem," the teenager said. "I already spent most of the money on a month of medicine for my momma. I got about fifty dollars left, Mr. Bodine, and you can have that back, but—"

"Here's what I'm thinking," Erhard cut in. "First of all, we see if we can't get Mrs. Waldron signed up for that Obamacare until she can find herself another job. I reckon she ought to qualify for some premium subsidies, which'll bring her insulin price back down to something she can manage."

"Premium subsidies," Bodine cackled. "Listen to you talk, Helmut. You sound like some kinda lawyer."

"And meanwhile, I figure Kevin can spend the rest of the summer helping out around this place. He puts in twenty hours a week at minimum wage, that ought to be worth a hundred bucks or so. By the time school starts up in September, he'll have paid y'all back, with money left over to help with the bills until his momma gets on her feet again."

"Could *use* a little he'p around the place, I guess," Bodine acknowledged. "I'm gittin' too *old* to handle this bidnis all by myself. I guess I could keep you on even *after* you go back to school, boy, you want to earn some extra spending money."

"How's that sound to you, Kevin?" asked Erhard.

"That sounds good, Mr. Erhard. That sounds *real* good."

Erhard turned to Bodine. "Arrangement seem all right to you, Frank?"

Josh Pachter

"Right as rain," the old man said. He went inside and scrabbled around in a storage closet at the back of the office, found a broom, came out and handed it to Kevin Waldron. "I reckon you might as well commence to sweepin' straight away, kid. This place ain't been swep' out since you was knee high to a grasshopper. Go on, now, git!"

A1A
Released 1974

"Making Music for Money"
"Door Number Three"
"Dallas"
"Presents to Send You"
"Stories We Could Tell"
"Life is Just a Tire Swing"
"A Pirate Looks at Forty"
"Migration"
"Trying to Reason With Hurricane Season"
"Nautical Wheelers"
"Tin Cup Chalice"

All songs by Jimmy Buffett,
except "Making Music for Money" (by Alex Harvey),
"Door Number Three" (with Steve Goodman),
"Dallas" (by Roger Bartlett),
and "Stories We Could Tell" (by John B. Sebastian).

A PIRATE LOOKS AT FORTY

Rick Ollerman

Charlie Stokes stood in the lee of the restaurant on Stock Island, watching the occasional car drive in or out of the asphalt parking lot. At seven o'clock, a shiny black SUV glided in and slid to an easy stop, its nose almost touching the faded board fence. Stokes checked his watch, though he knew what time it was; the man in the car was never late. It was more an excuse for Stokes to do something with his hands, to relieve the ache from a half hour of fruitless clenching and knuckle popping.

Stokes pushed off the wall and walked slowly to the vehicle, feeling the pounding beat of his pulse in his chest and temples. At the SUV, he pulled open the passenger door and climbed into the seat.

"Hello, Charlie."

Stokes did not look up. He kept his eyes forward, following the grain of the rough-hewn wooden slats through the windshield in front of them. "New car?"

"F-B-I special," the man said. "They like to give us new toys every once in a while. How've you been?"

"None of your business."

The man laughed quietly. He shifted in his seat to face Stokes. "Now that's where you're wrong, Charlie. You're exactly my business. You're why I'm here."

The washed-out color of the weathered fence took on a reddish hue as Stokes stared ahead, unblinking, eyes drying. Finally, he clamped them shut, feeling them burn, and said, "You killed my son."

"*He* drove the plane into that fuel truck, Charlie, not me."

"You were chasing him."

"He was running."

Stokes lashed out with a fist, denting the padding of the dashboard in front of him. "He hadn't done anything."

Blackledge shook his head slowly. He moved his hand to his waist. "He ran, Charlie. He shouldn't have done that."

Stokes closed his eyes again, now feeling the rush of blood in his ears. "What do you want from me?"

"I want you to keep your promise, Charlie. We have a deal. You tell us when somebody's using that airstrip of yours in the Bahamas, and we keep you out of jail."

"I've been doing that, haven't I?"

The leather upholstery creaked as Blackledge shifted his weight. "Well, that's just it, isn't it? Seems everything you've given us is stuff we already had, or else nothing we really cared about. There's some discussion you've been violating your plea deal, shirking your responsibility."

"My old friends have been a little leery since my arrest."

"It's been long enough. Ten years without parole—now *that's* a long time, isn't it? We gave you an opportunity, Charlie, because we thought it would work for us. Now you need to produce, or we will come down on you every bit as hard as we promised."

You already have, you bastard, Stokes thought. He was having a difficult time keeping his temper in check. He had to get out of the car. But he couldn't *think…*

"Might be something coming," he managed. "Soon."

"How soon?" asked Blackledge.

"As soon as I know, I'll tell you." Stokes pulled on the door latch, and the dusky evening air pushed into the air-conditioned

SUV, covering the sheen of sweat breaking out across his brow.

"Don't wait too long," Blackledge called.

Stokes slammed the door.

"Is Leon still in town?"

Stokes was behind the bar as Will and Jeff served the nighttime customers, the horde doing the "Duval crawl," hitting the joints up and down Key West's main party drag.

Jeff looked at Will, who was drawing a beer from the tap. Will shrugged, and Jeff said, "He was here yesterday. Lunchtime."

Stokes said, "Okay," meaning nothing in particular, and told the men he'd be back in a few hours. He'd worked out the handoff before his big arrest, Will and Jeff taking over the bar barely a month before the Feds would have seized it along with everything else. Everything they knew about, anyway, which was most things. Stokes rented a house from a real-estate management company, but what the FBI didn't know was that he owned it himself, like his last remaining boat, two items that had never had his name attached to any of their legal paperwork.

He knew where he'd find Leon. Whenever he came, either from the south of Colombia or Mexico City, Leon liked to throw his money at women, the ones who would straddle him over a chair and dance, mostly naked, in the VIP area of his favorite gentlemen's club.

The bouncer greeted him with a slapping handshake and a quick hug, loud pounding bass sounds and wispy clouds of cigarette smoke suffusing the small stand set up outside the front door. Three lingerie-clad ladies waved and smiled at the men coming up from the sidewalk.

"Been a while," the bouncer said. "Looking a little rough, Charlie. You here for a drink?"

"I feel like I've been drunk for two weeks already. More."

"Time to stop wishing and get to the fishing."

Stokes managed a smile. "Tonight, I'm just...looking for

someone." He turned and excused himself and edged past a group of young men waiting to pay the cover. "Hey, Nadine."

The woman, a dark-skinned Jamaican beauty, sashayed over, working her slender hips. "Hey, Charlie. Coming inside?"

"Not tonight, honey. Would you do an old pirate a favor?" He pulled a wad of bills from his pocket and separated out a ten-spot. "Friend of mine's inside. Could you get him for me?"

"You go in, Charlie. They'll let you."

Stokes shook off the offer. There was already too much noise in his head, and with the music and the dim red lighting...

"No, please," he said, "would you get him?" He described Leon's height, his shiny dark hair parted at the side, his penchant for wearing cream-colored shoes with no laces.

Nadine adjusted the sheer fabric over her enhanced chest and gave a small shrug and a practiced pout. "Okay," she said. "Hang loose." The words came out heavy with her native accent.

It took five minutes, but Nadine re-appeared with a short man, five-six, on her arm. Stokes reached into his pocket for another bill, but Leon beat him to it, inserting a twenty deftly between Nadine's breasts. "I like your outfit," he said, his own accent pronounced.

Nadine kissed him on the cheek. "Later, darling."

Stokes shuffled his feet, impatient, as Leon's eyes followed Nadine back to her spot beside the door, the curves of her dark skin called out by the white lace of her nightclothes. Then he turned: "What is so important, Charlie?"

The notion in Stokes's mind was inchoate but solidifying. "We need to talk."

Leon raised his eyebrows, half turning.

"Not in there," Stokes said. "Business."

"Oh, then, by all means, let us go."

They walked to the sidewalk then turned left, dodging a dwarf on a child's bicycle, a scarlet macaw perched on his shoulder.

* * *

Stokes went back to the bar the next day, just before noon. Will was changing beer kegs, and Jeff was stacking glasses behind the counter. A quarter of the tables, no more, had customers waiting for an early lunch. Two temporary local girls were the servers. Only two bar stools were occupied, near the end closest to Duval.

"Come over here," Stokes said to Jeff, moving to the far side, near the door to the kitchen.

"What's up, Charlie?"

Stokes's face was red. It wasn't from the heat, and it wasn't sunburn. "Feel like taking a little trip?"

Jeff looked behind him, said, "We don't need anything for today. Do we?"

"Not for the bar. I need you to make a Bahamas run."

Jeff leaned closer to Stokes, the bar top between them, and let his weight rest on his forearms. "We back in business?"

A quick nod.

"When?"

"Three days. Take the Beech."

"It's still at Homestead. Do you want it down here?"

"No, go from there. Make your stops but keep out of the Keys. We have fuel?"

"On the island? Should be two drums at least."

Stokes nodded. "Good. But there's something else."

"Sure, Charlie. What is it?"

"A little twist." Stokes lowered his voice and gave his instructions.

"We can't do that, Charlie. They'll kill you."

"Who will?"

"Both of them. Either of them. Does it matter?"

A fly landed on the back of Stokes's hand, and he shook it away without looking at it. There was soca music coming from the speakers above the bar. The fly buzzed near him again, and he made a grab for it.

Jeff said, "Is this about Phil?"

Stokes said nothing.

"He's gone, Charlie. We don't need to do this."

Stokes's face contorted, and tiny wrinkles like the surface of a sponge formed near the corners of his eyes. "Don't talk about my son."

Jeff straightened. "I—I'm sorry, Charlie."

"Will you do it?"

"Yeah, sure." Jeff shook his head, a new seriousness settling across his face like the shadow of an eclipse. "Of course, I'll do it."

"Thanks." Stokes cleared his throat. There was another buzz, but this time he made only a half-hearted wave at the insect. "Thank you."

This time they met on Big Coppitt Key. Stokes stood on the shore, squinting against the sun's glare off the water.

"Come on in," called Blackledge, who waded in flat water up to his knees. "Great day to be out here."

"Heard Mother Ocean's call, did you?"

"Lots of treasure out here. You always want to be a pirate, Charlie?"

"Since I was three feet tall."

"Plunder for the taking, right? I said come on in."

Stokes inserted his hands into the pockets of his shorts, looked down at his tanned feet ensconced in a pair of old Teva sandals. "I'll wait," he said.

"I want to help you, Charlie. I do." Blackledge said, not looking up from his reel, playing with the line. "There's some talk maybe you never *were* serious about our deal."

"What do *you* think?"

Blackledge shook his head. "Doesn't matter what I think. You take a man's money, his possessions—"

His son.

"—seems to me he'd like to keep what little he's got left. That's what I think." Now he did look up. "What do *you* think, Charlie?"

Stokes stood, squinting, keeping his thoughts to himself.

"I'm here to help you keep whatever you have left, Charlie. So come on out here and talk to me."

Stokes moved slowly. He stepped down the small bank and onto the spit of sand. His hands still in his pockets, not trusting them anywhere else, he waded into water, watching where he put each foot.

"So, Charlie," Blackledge said. "What have you got for me?"

"You doing all right, Charlie? You look like you're getting sick."

Stokes waved him off. "Just not sleeping too well, you know."

Jeff lowered his voice. "We still on for this weekend?"

"Too right," said Stokes. "You be there early, before sunup. Plane will be there about six, six-thirty."

"What is it? Cessna?"

A nod. "Two-oh-six. Nothing unusual."

They strolled down Eaton Street, past the Tropic Cinema. Dark now, the movies over, the place emptied out more than two hours ago.

"And the other stuff?"

Stokes gripped Jeff's shoulder, bringing him to a stop. "That's the most important thing. The most important thing in my life."

Jeff swallowed. He owed a lot to Charlie Stokes: money, kicks, women. Now, with the bar, the promise of an actual future. He just had to get past this weekend. "Okay, Charlie."

They resumed walking. A block behind them was a large shuffling crowd, but here, off the strip, it was almost dark, almost quiet. Jeff had the impression that Stokes was shrinking in the night air, like a cheap cotton T-shirt left too long in a dryer.

"I've got it covered, Charlie. The two-oh-six will come in, and we'll get it in the hangar. The pilot will lay over for, what? Three hours? More?"

51

"Leon said more. They don't want the plane in the States till after dark."

"Okay," Jeff said. "We'll have plenty of time, then. Maybe the pilot will take a nap."

"You can't count on that."

"I know, I know. Don't worry." A couple was coming toward them, heading northwest, arm in arm. Jeff waited until they were well past before continuing. "I'll get the other stuff tomorrow. Will's got the bar covered. When the pilot's in the building, we'll make the switch."

"He can't know."

Jeff shrugged. "We'll do our best."

"I know you will," said Stokes. He handed Jeff a piece of paper with Blackledge's license plate written on it, along with the make and color of his SUV. "There's something else. I'd like you to find this car. Should be at one of the hotels."

Jeff glanced at the paper and shoved it into his pocket. "Do I want to know?"

"You do not. Try the best resorts first. Look at night: I don't know where it'll be during the day."

"Okay, Charlie." Jeff felt he should argue or resist, but he merely walked on. Then he went back to their original topic: "How long you want me to stay on the island?"

"An hour after he leaves. Then get back here with the cargo. Blackledge's people will already be on Leon's guy."

"Got it. There's just…"

"What?"

"You're sure you want to do this?"

"Oh, yeah," said Charlie. "I'm sure." He scratched a patch of gray stubble on the side of his jaw, and the two men continued on, each contemplating a possible version of the future and wondering if the other would be in it.

Charlie Stokes and Emily McNee walked—everyone walks in

Key West—to Mallory Square, contemplative in their quiet. There were no cruise ships docked yet. Emily checked her watch and nudged Stokes with her shoulder. "Should be a ship in a half hour. We don't want to be here, do we?"

"Hmm?"

"What's wrong, Charlie? I haven't seen you all week, and you're just so...out of it."

Stokes blinked behind his sunglasses, studying the gulls waddling around a puddle on the concrete in front of them. He turned to Emily, smiling. "This is why I go for younger women. Everything's always good with you."

"Stop that."

"What?"

"Forcing that heinous fake smile on your face. I swear you've made more new wrinkles this week than you have in the five years I've known you." Then, after a pause, "Is it your son?"

He nodded, his eyes hidden by his glasses.

"I wish I'd known him better."

"I know." Stokes's cheeks relaxed, and he exhaled. "Thank you. Sometimes..."

"Shh," Emily said. "That's better. Now when are you going to tell me what's going on?"

He touched her elbow. "Let's go down to Freeman's."

"The jeweler's?"

"Mm-hmm."

"Going to buy me something pretty?"

"Whatever you like." They turned away from the water, taking a crooked and easy line through the clumping groups of visitors. "I need you to do something for me."

"What's that?"

He told her. Her face went pale in the bright sunshine. "You've never asked me to...be part of that life. You've never even talked about it."

Stokes shrugged, helpless. "I can't do it myself. They see me with a shovel, they'll send an army."

53

"Who will?"

He shrugged again. "I'm probably being watched."

Emily couldn't help herself—she turned around, quickly at first, then slowing as she came back to face him.

"I'll do it," she said. "It's just three coffee cans?"

He touched her elbow again. It was a natural gesture between them, these casual touches, and it was a communication. "They're heavy. You'll have to make trips."

"You need them tonight?"

"I do."

"Okay, Charlie, I'll do it. You know, this is the first thing you've ever asked me to do."

They arrived at Freeman's Gold Studio. Stokes held the door for Emily. A man sat behind a row of display cases, wearing glasses and holding a small torch over a vise. When he saw Stokes and Emily, he snapped off the torch and said, "Charlie! Come in, come in."

"How are you, Oscar?"

"Good. You looking for something?"

"Just you. Got a minute?"

Oscar Freeman looked at Emily, and Stokes told her, "Find something you like."

"Don't be silly," she said. "But I'll look."

The two men disappeared through a doorway. "You want the money?" said Freeman. He gestured toward the large safe set against the far corner of the room.

"I will," said Stokes. "Tomorrow." He told Freeman about the coffee cans. "And that's it. This'll be the last of it."

"No more gold, then?"

"Not from me. Come on," Stokes said, almost smiling. "You've been melting my Krugerrands for long enough. Now you'll have to get a legitimate supply."

"But then I stop paying you."

"It was never meant to last, Oscar. Over the last five years, you've made enough money to buy Miami. It's been good."

And it had been, for both of them, with Stokes supplying gold coins for Freeman to melt and use in his jewelry. As the pieces were sold in the shop, Stokes took his percentage and nobody was the wiser.

"Okay, Charlie. And after tomorrow?"

"I'll probably piss my share away," said Stokes. "We'll see."

"Will we?" asked Freeman.

Stokes clapped his friend on the back. "Come out front. Emily needs something nice."

"On the house, of course."

"Of course," Stokes said.

They met for the final time two blocks north of the Southernmost Point buoy marker. Stokes climbed into the black SUV, rousing Blackledge from his heat-induced torpor. Once Stokes shut the door, Blackledge started the vehicle, putting the open driver's side window up and cranking the A/C.

"So it's on," Blackledge started.

Stokes said nothing.

"I'm glad you're doing this, Charlie. It's the right decision."

Stokes stared through the windshield at the anonymous cars parked along the street in front of them. "What decision?" he said. "We have a deal."

"And you don't want to go to prison."

"No. I don't want to go to prison."

Stokes had the sense Blackledge was smiling. Something in the voice, maybe. He felt the muscles tighten across his chest.

"I'm flying out this afternoon," said Blackledge. "But I'll be back. Then we'll have another talk."

"What for?"

"Because, Charlie. Because. You want to keep walking free, you have to pay the toll. So we'll be talking."

"Go to hell."

"Charlie—"

"Shut up," Stokes said, opening his door and climbing down. He slammed it shut as Blackledge lowered the window.

"That's not a healthy attitude, Charlie."

Through curled lips, Stokes said, "We'll talk about it when you come back." *You presenting baboon,* he thought, and walked off.

The FBI man put his SUV in gear and eased out of his parking spot along the curb.

He's going to hurt himself, Blackledge thought. *Just like his boy did.*

At the bar Thursday night, Jeff took the stool next to Stokes.

"You find that car?"

"You were right," said Jeff. "He's at Grand Key."

"Thank you."

"No problem, Charlie." He lowered his voice to a whisper. "Anything else? Before I take off?"

"We're good, I think."

"Okay, man." Jeff patted his friend on the arm and stood. "You better know what you're doing, Charlie. You can't screw these guys any bigger than this."

Stokes nodded and picked up his beer. He held it in front of him, examining the bubbles as they broke away from the inside of the glass and rose to the surface. Then he put it down without drinking and watched over his shoulder as Jeff exited the bar. He had to find Leon next.

Actually, he thought, *I need to* survive *Leon next.*

He waved Will over. "There's a cell phone in the lost-and-found box," he said. "Hand it over."

It was a burner Stokes had paid cash for the day before, at a drugstore on Duval. He dialed a number from memory.

"Hello?"

"Leon."

"What's wrong?"

"Nothing," Charlie said. "Everything's set."

"Then why the hell are you calling me? You don't do that, man. Not unless there's something going down." Anger was building in Leon's voice.

"Tomorrow," said Stokes. "I need to see you."

"No, no," Leon said. "You will be paid the same way—"

"It's not that." Stokes named a restaurant. "I'll be at a booth in the back, away from the door."

"What is going on, Charlie?"

"Nothing that can't wait till then. But you'll want to see me."

"You're making me—"

Stokes pressed a button and hung up. He tossed the phone to Will and told him to put it back in the lost and found.

"Where are you going?"

"Anywhere but here," Stokes answered. "And you haven't seen me."

Will tossed him a quick salute and hurried off to fill an order.

"Take it easy, my friend," Stokes said quietly.

The next morning, Leon slid into the booth across from Stokes. His features were contorted, and Stokes was gratified that the man could contain himself enough to speak quietly.

"What are you doing, Charlie? Huh?" Leon leaned far over the table, using it as a barrier to help his control.

"I'll—"

"Do you have a gun, Charlie? Do you?" Leon moved his right arm to his hip. "I do, Charlie."

"Leon, relax. Please."

"Do not tell me to relax. You know what happened last night, don't you? At the airport in Homestead."

Where Philip had died. Been killed…

"Where's your pilot?"

"I don't give a damn about the pilot."

"Did they arrest him?"

"They took him away. They still have him. That's not the problem. Where is the freaking cargo, Charlie? Eh? It was on the plane when it left for your airstrip. When it got to the States, though, it had turned into something else, some kind of construction material."

"Gypsum," Stokes said.

"What?"

"It's gypsum. They use it in construction. For walls."

Leon's hand came away from his hip, out from under his untucked shirt. Stokes heard a hard thump against the underside of the table.

"So it was you? You are going to—"

"Leon, stop!" Stokes' voice was harsh. The approaching waitress backed away, giving the two gentlemen at her table some space.

"What have you done, Charlie?"

"I saved your ass, that's what I've done. The stuff is safe."

"What are you talking about?"

"I know where your cargo is. And who has it."

"You better explain. Quickly."

Stokes described a black SUV, along with its plate number, and told Leon where it could be found.

"A hotel parking lot? And it has all of...all the packages?"

Stokes nodded. "It's all there. The man who owns the car will be back this morning."

"He is stealing from us?"

He stole from me, Stokes thought. "That's why he came to town."

Leon kept his hand low, out of sight. "Why all this? Why the switch?"

Stokes shrugged. "I didn't know what he was up to. Then I found out. Now I'm talking to you. You going to take care of it?"

Leon's hand returned to his waistband. He smoothed his shirt and pulled a cell phone from his trouser pocket. "Oh, yes,

I will take care of it. If this is not as you say—"

"Relax, Leon." Stokes exhaled. "We have a deal, don't we?"

"A deal," repeated Leon, dialing.

Stokes slid out from the booth as Leon spoke in rapid-fire Spanish. He dropped a bill on the table and waited.

"I have to go," said Leon, moving quickly.

"This Blackledge, guy who owns the car. You know he's government?"

"Who cares?"

"Just making sure you're aware. When he gets back—"

"—he will cease to be a problem," Leon said simply.

For both of us.

The Colombian turned and left the restaurant at a near run.

Stokes answered the waitress's raised eyebrows with a reassuring smile, but inside he felt the tension drain from his features. "Have a good day," he said.

Outside, there was no sign of Leon. Across the street in a parking lot, a white Chevrolet waited with its windows down. Emily McNee sat behind the wheel.

"Everything go okay?" she asked, as Stokes lowered himself into the passenger seat.

"So far," he answered. "Things will be better when we're on the boat."

And out of territorial waters.

Emily started the car. "How are you?"

He sat back and closed his eyes behind his sunglasses and wondered where Special Agent Blackledge was at precisely that moment.

He thought of things undone and wrongs redressed.

Revenge. Payback.

He thought of his son, Philip, and of what might have been.

Redemption.

"You sure you're ready to leave the Keys, Charlie?"

"I'm over forty. My occupational hazards caught up with me long ago."

"A victim of fate. That sounds so sad. You're not giving up, are you? Is that what you're doing? With me?"

"No, no." He patted her leg. "I don't mean it like that. More like I've had enough of the wrong kind of adventure. We'll do something new."

"The two of us? You ready for that?"

Stokes didn't answer. After a couple of minutes, Emily looked over to see if he was sleeping.

He wasn't. "When you're younger," he said, "everything's always about *later*. The *future*. There's always tomorrow."

"Is this about your son?" said Emily.

Stokes let out a long breath. "You know what maturity is? It's realizing there's no such thing as tomorrow. You've already made all your choices. All the big ones, anyway."

"Charlie, you're scaring me."

"The cannons don't thunder anymore. It happens. You have my passport?"

"In my bag. Charlie, what have you done?"

"I made a choice. I've done something I didn't think I could do."

Emily said, not understanding, "That's so sweet."

He smiled. "I'm glad you think so."

"Another island, another country," Emily said, checking over her shoulder and driving on.

Charlie leaned back against the passenger headrest. "Yeah, something like that."

Changes in Latitudes, Changes in Attitudes
Released 1977

"Changes in Latitudes, Changes in Attitudes"
"Wonder Why We Ever Go Home"
"Banana Republics"
"Tampico Trauma"
"Lovely Cruise"
"Margaritaville"
"In the Shelter"
"Miss You So Badly"
"Biloxi"
"Landfall"

All songs by Jimmy Buffett,
except "Banana Republics"
(by Jim Rothermel and Steve Goodman),
"Lovely Cruise" (by Jonathan Baham),
"Miss You So Badly" (with Greg "Fingers" Taylor),
and "Biloxi" (by Jesse Winchester).

TAMPICO TRAUMA

Michael Bracken

Sometimes the worm at the bottom of a tequila bottle is the only protein a man needs to see himself through the night. At least, that's what I told myself until I awoke to a bloodshot Tampico morning and found one of three señoritas force-feeding me *huevos rancheros,* refried beans, and corn tortillas.

"*¿Como esta, Capitain?*"

Maria, Gabriela, and Veronica Hernández had asked the same question every morning since they dragged me off the beach, my arms wrapped around a shrink-wrapped cube of cash, a bullet hole through my left thigh. Maria, by four years the eldest of the three sisters, found me just before dawn and enlisted the assistance of her sisters to get me from the beach to their adobe casa a half mile away.

Less than a year separated the two younger women, and they could so easily have been twins that I repeatedly mistook one for the other until I realized Veronica was the only one who spoke English with any fluency. The bullet hole in my thigh, the cube of cash, and all their new apparel purchased with money from the cube told them everything they needed to know about me. What I learned about them during my recuperation was their intense interest in the United States of America. I didn't know much about my home country. Until I started running

63

dope up from Mexico, I'd never even left Texas.

I was lucid enough that first morning to refuse medical treatment, fearing a doctor's visit would lead to my discovery, and I relied on the nursing skills of the three sisters and the medicinal properties of agave. Tequila wasn't the only oral painkiller available, though, as the women proved repeatedly while they nursed me back to health, and they were always careful not to disturb the bandages they had wrapped around my thigh. With three pretty señoritas who catered to my every need, I swore I would never return home.

Late one night, after I was finally able to get out of bed and limp around the casa, the youngest sister brought home a squat brown-skinned man with a bristly black moustache and an ill-fitting uniform identifying him as an officer in the Policía Federal Ministerial. A black leather holster strapped to his belt held a long-barreled revolver, and the holster was nearly as dusty as his black boots. He pulled up a chair and sat across the table from me. "You look like you need a friend."

"You look like you need a drink," I said in return.

I caught the attention of one of the sweet chiquitas, held up my glass and the index finger of my other hand. A moment later an empty glass appeared before him, and I filled it and mine with the last of the tequila from the bottle I'd been nursing since sundown.

He ignored his drink. "There are some very bad men looking for a gringo who fits your description. If I were your friend, I could make them look elsewhere."

By the time President Nixon's War on Drugs began, Earl Grissom had been moving marijuana from Tampico into Corpus Christi for nearly two years, and I had been part of his crew for almost as long. Grissom bought the marijuana from Mexican villagers who ferried it down the Pánuco River in fifty-pound burlap sacks that were loaded onto his boat in the dead of night under the watchful eye of well-paid Mexican Federales. Several days later, we unloaded the bales in a waterfront warehouse near

Corpus Christi and returned south with cubes of cash. We were paid well for our efforts, but a few of my former crewmates had made mistakes and had seen their travels end in the middle of the Gulf. The longer the operation ran, the more paranoid Grissom became, and the more I realized we needed to part company.

One sweltering July night, when I thought the rest of the crew weren't looking, I took a cube and jumped ship. I thought I'd made a clean getaway until I heard shouting and gunshots and the tiny splashes of bullets peppering the water around me.

I had never seen the Federale now sitting across from me at the loading dock when we were collecting our north-bound cargo, so I didn't know what to expect. I leaned forward. "And what would it take to be your friend?"

He smiled then, a gold tooth flashing reflected candlelight. "My sister tells me you've been quite generous."

I glanced at the three women hovering around us. "Which one?"

He smiled again. "Veronica."

I considered the women huddled on the far side of the room and could not see a family resemblance. They were full-breasted and wide-hipped, with caramel skin and raven black hair that fell well below their shoulders. What differentiated them from their older brother was attitude. His was ugly. And he was awaiting my response.

The cube of cash I'd taken off the boat had long since been broken open and the contents hidden in the false bottom of the older sister's armoire, and that the Federale hadn't gone directly to it told me what I needed to know about his sisters. I dug in my pants pocket, found a pair of crumpled Benjamin Franklins, and tossed them on the table. "Perhaps you could get a haircut and a shave," I suggested. "Maybe get your uniform cleaned and pressed."

After the money disappeared into his pocket, the Federale said, "That's a start, my friend, but the gentlemen looking for you tell my superior that you took much more from them than this."

"And you believe them?"

He smiled again. "How could I not?"

"How could you not," I agreed.

The Federale lifted his glass and drained the tequila in one swift swallow. Then he stood. "I shall return another day to continue our new friendship."

As the door closed behind him, Veronica rushed to my side. "I'm sorry," she said. "Raphael made me bring him here."

"How could he do that?"

She pulled up her sleeve and showed me the fingertip-sized bruises on her forearm. "My brother is a cruel man. He saw me paying for your tequila with American dollars. He took the money and made me tell him where I had gotten it."

"And you told him I was here?"

Veronica nodded.

"So I've no reason to hide," I said as I examined the bottom of the bottle, "and I've no more tequila."

She shook her head.

"Where's the nearest bar?"

Veronica refused to answer my question, so I asked her sisters. "*¿Dónde está la cantina más cercana?*"

Maria smiled and helped me to my feet. Before we reached the door, the three sisters began to argue. I could not understand everything they said, but I caught the gist of it. Veronica told the others that it was not safe for me to leave, and Maria, who ultimately won the argument, insisted nothing bad would happen as long as I was with her, because in this part of Tampico everyone knew their brother. That seemed to end the discussion, and soon the two of us made our way along a dirt road to a cantina where I was the only gringo in the place.

She brought a bottle of tequila from the bar and helped me drink it, taking one shot for every three of mine. When much of the bottle was empty, she asked, "*¿Por qué estás aquí? ¿De qué te escondes? ¿Qué quieres de nosotros?*" Why are you here? What are you hiding from? What do you want from us?

Philosophical discussions were beyond me whenever I had a belly full of tequila serving as a dead worm's swimming pool. Years earlier, I had dropped out of college to hustle pot in Corpus Christi. Before long, I was using my sailing experience to import it, and what began as youthful indiscretion became a lifestyle in which I was in constant danger of being dumped overboard in the middle of the Gulf. I had jumped ship in Tampico intending to use the money I took to get lost somewhere in Mexico, but all I managed to do was hole up with the three beautiful sisters of a Federale who could drop me in a Mexican prison any time he tired of our friendship.

I told her none of this. Instead, I said, "You dragged me off the beach. What do *you* want?"

She lowered her voice and leaned forward. *"¿Puedes ayudarnos a escapar de mi hermano?"* Can you help us escape my brother?

"Why?"

She stared into my eyes. "You saw how he is. He is like that always, taking what is not his, even from us."

"And yet you told him nothing about the money."

"He would take it, and it is not his."

I lifted my hand and motioned for a replacement bottle.

"No," she said as she clasped my arm and drew it down to the table. "We will return home, and I will tend to your needs, and you will see to ours."

I leaned heavily on Maria on the way back to the casa, as much from the effect of the tequila as from the still-healing wound in my thigh.

The next morning, as every morning, I awoke to find one of the señoritas force-feeding me *huevos rancheros,* refried beans, and corn tortillas.

"¿Como esta, Capitain?"

I pushed away a forkful of eggs and stared at the señorita

feeding me. I thought I was seeing double until the one on the left—the middle sister—spoke.

"Maria said you would help us escape," Gabriela said. "She took some of the money to get us passports."

I didn't remember agreeing to that. I didn't remember much of anything after she put me to bed. I said, "Won't your brother find out?"

"My sister knows a man who can keep secrets."

"Who is this man?" I asked. "What does he do?"

"Father Miguel."

"A priest?"

"Who better?" She smiled. "He was Maria's lover before he took the vows. He would do anything for her, and he has no love for my brother."

I pondered that in my early morning state.

The Federale reappeared a few nights later, joining me at my table in the cantina with an empty glass he had taken from the bar. I was drinking alone because his sisters had gone to evening mass without me. His uniform had been cleaned and pressed, and his boots shined. Even his black leather holster showed signs of care.

"We have much to celebrate, my friend," he said. He poured himself a drink from my bottle and pointed to the new insignia on his lapel. "You *are* still my friend, eh?"

"Of course I am."

"You think it is safe for you to be seen like this? Do you not think the bad men will find you?"

I smiled though a tequila fog and rested my hand on his forearm. "I think my new friend will protect me."

He pulled his arm away. "Perhaps."

Several Benjamin Franklins made their way from my pocket to his.

"Why are these bad men so intent on finding you? What is it

that you have that they want?"

"Your sisters," I told him, lifting my tequila in a toast.

"Bah!" he said. He fingered the money, silently counting it. "You are a fool. How little you value our friendship."

I patted my pockets, making a big show of searching for more money I knew I didn't have.

He swatted the shot glass from my hand, stood, and marched out of the cantina.

The next night, all three of the sisters joined me at the cantina for tacos and tequila. They had cut my hair and given me a shave, my first since landing on the beach, and I wore loose-fitting bell-bottoms one of the sisters had purchased at the market to replace the pants they had cut off me weeks earlier. They wore colorful skirts and white blouses, and they had piled their hair atop their heads and festooned it with fresh flowers. We ate and we drank, and we laughed and celebrated their successful acquisition of passports.

"You're certain your brother doesn't know?"

"Our secret is in the hands of God," said the middle sister. "He will protect us."

Our celebration ended when a heavily bearded gringo built like the defensive lineman he had once been stared in the window and grinned. A moment later, Earl Grissom entered the cantina, wrapped a meaty fist around my shirt, and lifted me from my seat.

"That smarmy little son-of-a-bitch said you couldn't be found," he said. I had watched Grissom dump bodies into the Gulf to feed the sharks and knew that no one ever wanted to be his chum. "All the while he kept directing us to other parts of Tampico. I began to wonder why."

"That little Federale is more than a friend," I said, waving at the three sisters still sitting around the table. "He's practically family."

I wrapped my fist around the neck of the tequila bottle I had been nursing. I swung it hard and fast, and, though I didn't accomplish my goal when I hit him, Grissom did release his grip on my shirt and stumble back several steps.

The hole in my thigh had damaged more than my smooth skin, and I had yet to regain complete mobility. So I barely kept my feet beneath me and only managed *that* by grabbing the back of my chair. I motioned for the sisters to move away.

"No one steals from me," Grissom said. "You should know that."

The other drinkers vacated the surrounding tables, pressing back against the walls of the cantina or slipping out the door behind Grissom.

He snapped open a switchblade and rushed me. The blade tore a gash in my shirt as I stepped aside. I still held the tequila bottle, and I swung it hard at his wrist, hoping to knock the knife from his fist. As before, I failed, and he stabbed at me again.

I pushed the chair between us, and he tore it from my grip. I balanced on my good leg and awaited the inevitable.

A gunshot stopped both of us, and I turned to see my Federale friend standing in the cantina doorway, his long-barreled revolver in his hand. He examined me and said, "I am disappointed in you, my friend. What has happened here?"

Neither Grissom nor I spoke, but the bartender, who had been tipped quite handsomely each night he served me, explained in a rushed voice that I had been attacked.

Raphael looked me in the eye and told me to take his sisters home. "You have caused enough trouble here."

I waved a thumb at my former employer. "What about him?"

The Federale smiled. "I know just the place for him."

Grissom protested. "You can't do anything to me. I pay the Commandant—"

"The Commandant has gone missing," Raphael said with a twisted smile. His gold tooth glinted in the dim light, and he pointed at the new insignia on his lapel. "I'm in charge now, and we have much to discuss if you wish to be my friend."

The sisters and I had been back in their casa for less than an hour when their brother and two other Federales pushed their way inside. Raphael said, "It is time to go."

I looked up at him as his two companions grabbed my arms. "I thought you were my friend."

"Friendships come and friendship go, gringo," he said. "I have a new friend now, and he values our friendship far more than you ever did."

The three men dragged me out of the sisters' home, into the center of the dusty street. Raphael left me under the watchful eyes of the other two Federales and disappeared into the casa.

I heard arguing from within, the sounds of flesh striking flesh and furniture breaking. I stepped forward, intending to protect the sisters as best I could, but I was stopped by a firm grip on my arm. Soon the newly promoted Federale exited the casa, a fistful of Benjamin Franklins in one fist.

"My sisters did not give up your money without coercion," he said, "but this is all I found."

Over his shoulder, I saw the oldest sister step into the doorway, her clothes torn, her nose bleeding, the flowers ripped from her hair. She had her arm wrapped around Veronica, who was crying into her shoulder. Gabriela stood beside them and looked no better.

I started to speak, but Maria held up her hand and shook her head to silence me. Before I could do anything more, the three men formed a semi-circle behind me and Raphael kicked the back of my left leg, dropping me to my knees.

He drew his sidearm and pressed the revolver's barrel against the back of my head. He squeezed the trigger, and I voided a night of drinking as the hammer snapped down on an empty chamber.

They laughed and then dragged me down to the docks,

where a cargo ship was making ready to leave port. They dumped me at the foot of the ship's gangway, and the Federale leaned down to whisper in my ear, so close his bristly moustache tickled me as he spoke.

"I let you live only for my sisters," he said. He shoved an unopened bottle of tequila in my hand. "Leave now, my friend. If you return, I may not continue to pretend that your miserable life has value."

I realized I looked a mess, but I pulled myself to my feet and ascended the gangway before turning back. I could see the three sisters in the distance, and I knew the Catholic priest held their passports and much of the money I had given them for their travels. I hoped their brother would not find it.

The next night, I sat in the ship's canteen and shared my last bottle of tequila with my new shipmates, regaling them with tales of my drug-running adventures and the healing ministrations of the three sisters. I had been travelling quite a bit and was ready to return home to Corpus Christi, where I hoped the sisters might someday find me.

I upended the bottle, sucked down the worm with the last swallow of tequila, and lifted the empty bottle in mock salute.

Sometimes you eat the worm. Sometimes you *are* the worm.

Hidey ho, boys!

Son of a Son of a Sailor
Released 1978

"Son of a Son of a Sailor"
"Fool Button"
"The Last Line"
"Livingston Saturday Night"
"Cheeseburger in Paradise"
"Coast of Marseilles"
"Cowboy in the Jungle"
"Mañana"
"African Friend"

All songs by Jimmy Buffett,
except "The Last Line" and
"Coast of Marseilles" (both by Keith Sykes).

CHEESEBURGER IN PARADISE

Don Bruns

Muenster, Iowa: sleepy, middle of nowhere, population three hundred and two. By tomorrow, that number would be one less, assuming Ginger Gallagher accomplished his mission, killed Jamie Muenster, made the whole thing look like an accident. Piece of cake.

Ginger took a bite of his cheeseburger and wiped his mouth with a paper napkin. For a small town, the Paradise Café had a decent menu and a pretty good cheeseburger, smashed down flat on the grill, just a little char on the outside. The Paradise advertised its fresh beef came from two hundred yards away. You could see cows in a pen outside the restaurant window, a slaughterhouse just down the road. There was "farm to table," and then there was "meet your meal." This was definitely the latter. Creepy.

"More coffee, hon?"

The wrinkled waitress had her gray hair in a bun and a vacant stare in her eyes, resigned to living out her remaining years taking orders for cheeseburgers and more coffee.

"Sure."

Jamie Muenster was the son of William Muenster, who was the son of Myron Von Muenster, who was the son of...well, it just kept going back, seven or eight generations, to the town's

75

founding. Jamie ate lunch at the Paradise every Wednesday, regular as clockwork. This was Wednesday, and Ginger was about to get his first look at his target.

He'd seen photos, press clippings, news stories. Now it was time to see the man close up, observe any frailties, any traits, anything that might give Ginger an idea how to kill the man in a manner that would convince the law his death had been purely accidental.

Or, if that turned out to be impractical, how to just shoot the guy. One clean shot to the brain or heart and make a clean get-away.

Ginger preferred an accident. But his assignment was to produce a dead body. The how was left to his discretion.

Muenster's nearest neighbor, Clear Lake, was famous for three deaths that had happened in 1959, when a plane crash killed Buddy Holly, Ritchie Valens, and the Big Bopper, recording artists who had just finished a concert at the Surf Ballroom. Ginger didn't think he could arrange a plane crash for Jamie Muenster. Too much choreography. Too expensive. But the idea of a vehicular accident intrigued him.

He sipped coffee and studied his phone. A man sitting by himself and staring at the door would be suspect. But a man studying his phone, occasionally picking it up and talking into it, punching buttons, well, that was the most normal thing in the world.

He took another bite of burger, washed it down with more of the slightly bitter black liquid. Last thing he wanted to do was stand out.

Hitman Rule Number Ten: Don't stand out.

He punched random numbers and letters. Most normal thing in the world.

The door swung open, and a blonde in tight, ripped jeans, maybe thirty years old, entered, followed by a lean, tanned cowboy in worn jeans, plaid work shirt, neckerchief and gray ten-gallon hat, sporting a worn leather holster holding what appeared to be a nine-millimeter Smith and Wesson.

Third through the door came a short, stout, pudgy-faced man with greased-back black hair. He wore a shabby gray suit that hung on him rather than fit him. He was dabbing at his face with a white handkerchief.

Jamie Muenster and his posse had arrived.

Nodding at the four tables of diners and smiling at the lunch-counter crowd, Muenster followed the girl and the cowboy to a red-vinyl corner booth. He let the two of them sit beside each other and perched across from them, glancing around the room, checking the tables, ready for a quick exit if need be. His eyes rested briefly on Gallagher, noting a stranger in the room. In this burg, any strange face would be suspect.

Jamie, Ginger had learned, owned a farm-implement business outside Clear Lake and was honorary mayor of the town that bore his ancestor's name. He should have been *the* big shot in the community. But he wasn't. The big shot was Casper Roulan, a wealthy cattle rancher whose son Jared had been arrested for rape and manslaughter. Roulan and Jared were famous, these days, though not as famous as the son's alleged victim, Sophia Sanchez, daughter of a Mexican drug runner, Iowa State Fair beauty queen, news anchor on KIMT in Mason City. The Sanchez case was getting national attention.

Jamie Muenster was going to testify for the prosecution, scheduled to take the stand at the Cerro Gordo County Court House in Mason City on Friday, and there were those who were not happy about it, Casper Roulan in particular. Muenster was well aware someone might try to stop him, but, despite the glance, Ginger was pretty sure Muenster had no idea it was supposed to be him.

The girl ordered a salad with chicken, the cowboy asked for a chipotle bean burrito, and Jamie Muenster said he'd have a cheeseburger. Lettuce, tomato, an onion slice, Heinz 57 sauce, kosher dill pickle on the side. "Burn it, Erma," the man said. "You know how I like it."

This might just be your last meal, old man, Ginger thought. *A cheeseburger at the Paradise Café.*

Rich boy Jared and the lady reporter had apparently been a hot item for a short time. Reports of Jared's infidelities, his displays of temper, and at least two illegitimate children apparently changed her mind, and she left the rancher's son and teamed up with her co-anchor. Next thing you knew, her body was found in a cornfield, raped and strangled. The co-anchor had an iron-clad alibi: he'd been five hundred miles away on assignment in Toledo, Ohio, doing a story on a javelin thrower who was a late qualifier for the Olympics.

The ex-boyfriend was the logical next suspect, but he was the fair-haired son of the most influential man in Muenster, so no one wanted to make that accusation. Until Jamie announced he might have seen the couple together the night of the murder. He should have kept his mouth shut. Would have extended his life expectancy.

Cops got a warrant to search Jared's tricked-out Ford F150 and found fingerprints, hair, even a few specks of blood that all traced back to Sophia Sanchez. That and Jamie's eyewitness account led to an arrest and indictment.

Ginger looked around the café. The folks at the booths and tables had gone quiet when the threesome walked in, but now there was a buzz, a lot of nodding and leaning in for quiet conversation.

Jared Roulan was out on a million-dollar bail bond. His dad had mortgaged the ranch to come up with the hundred thousand it took to arrange the bond. If Jared had joined Casper and his posse for lunch, there would have been a lot more commotion. Half the town was financially involved with the Roulans, the other half resented the special perks to which the cattle baron's wealth entitled him. If Jared killed the girl, they thought, he ought to be convicted.

The boy's fate pretty much hinged on the testimony of one man: Jamie Muenster. He'd spotted Jared's F150, he told the police, the night Sophia Sanchez was murdered. It was parked just off Seward Road on a desolate grassy field, and Jamie had pulled up to the open driver's window and asked if everything was all right.

Two people had been in the vehicle, and Jamie was pretty sure the passenger was the Sanchez woman. He watched her almost every night on TV, and she was easy to recognize. Jared, he said, had assured him everything was just fine.

Of course, Jared denied Jamie's story. Sure, Sophia's hair, fingerprints and DNA were in his truck. He'd dated her for several months. She'd been in the truck many times, cut her finger once, that explained the blood. Jared said he never parked with her on Seward Road, not the night she died, not ever. They'd broken up. She had a new boyfriend. He was out of the picture.

The rape kit was inconclusive—the attacker had worn a condom—and the girl was strangled with a cloth, not bare hands. But Jamie stuck to his story. Without his testimony, there would be no case against Jared Roulan.

Enter Ginger Gallager.

Thirty thousand dollars was his asking price, though he figured he could have held out for fifty.

Whenever Ginger was ready for a new assignment, he'd buy a burner phone and take out a classified in the *Chicago Trib*. Buried in the ad would a long string of numbers, his phone number spaced out with a certain code.

Then he waited. Could be hours, could be weeks. Eventually, Paladin would call. He would name a target. Ginger had twenty-four hours to accept or decline.

Only four soldiers out of his class of forty-six had made it out of the Fort Benning sniper school. The other forty-two washed out. During his hitch, Ginger had racked up thirty kills. Then, when he got out, there'd been a vague email, an unlisted number phone number to call, and Paladin's guarantee of at least five hundred thousand a year. He'd never met Paladin face to face. Over the three years of his employment, Ginger had become proficient in knives, poisons, traffic accidents…the list went on.

But the options in Muenster seemed limited. Small town, few opportunities. Still, thirty thousand for a three-day assignment? Not a bad paycheck. String together twenty of those a year, and that was pretty good money.

Ginger focused on the blonde. Daughter? Secretary? Lover? The cowboy eating the bean burrito was probably a bodyguard. He hoped there wouldn't be collateral damage. It was messy when peripheral people had to be killed. He'd managed to avoid that over his last seven missions. If you planned carefully, you could usually isolate the target. That was always Ginger's intent. But you never knew.

He paid for his burger and coffee with cash, left a twenty percent tip. Hitman Rule Number Eight: Never use credit, never tip too much or too little. Blend in. Don't leave a lasting impression.

Most of the rules boiled down to the same thing.

Ginger waited a block from the Paradise Café. With his Upland 10x42mm binoculars, his view of the victim's black Lincoln Navigator was perfect. When Jamie exited the restaurant, it would be easy to pop him with a high-powered rifle, but that wasn't how this was going to play out. People on the street would panic, the local-yokel cops would quickly block the roads leading out of the small town.

Small towns were a bitch. In New York, Chicago, LA, you could do your job and be swallowed up by the metropolis in seconds. In Muenster, Iowa, it would be hard to hide.

He watched Jamie, the cowboy and the blonde come out of the Paradise. The cowboy did a quick perimeter check, and so did Jamie. Ginger was certain his target was even more cautious than the man in the ten-gallon hat. After all, it was *his* life that was at stake.

The threesome stepped into the Lincoln, and Ginger started his rental Hyundai, easing out of its parking spot with two or three bucks left on the meter. Parking meters in Muenster, Iowa. Who the hell had dreamed *that* up? Hardly anyone lived here. But all he needed was a parking ticket to screw up his mission. Muenster fucking Iowa. He couldn't wait to get out of this speck on the map.

The Lincoln made a single stop: liquor store, probably the only one in town. The girl walked in, leaving Jaime in the car with the suntanned cowboy. Ten minutes later, she came out with a bag of bottles. They were either headed for a party or back to Jamie's place. Maybe a party *at* Jamie's place. If the cowboy was a constant, this was going to be tough. Ginger needed to separate the gun-toting bodyguard from his mark. And soon.

He followed at a respectable distance. A dozen houses close together, then bigger homes on bigger lots. Finally, a mile down Sunflower Boulevard, the Navigator pulled into a driveway. The afternoon sun highlighted a large brick home, probably the estate of the town's namesake. Impressive, with a wrap-around porch and a manicured lawn.

When the trio were inside the house, Ginger contemplated the Navigator. It was unlikely there were security cameras in the trees, so the vehicle was fair game. He could cut the brake lines or attach an explosive device to the starter, not that hard to do. But Cowboy seemed to be the primary driver. If he got sent out on his own for coffee in the morning, his death would serve no purpose.

Figuring they were tucked away for the rest of the day, Ginger headed back into town. He drove past the Paradise and hung a left onto First Street, the only numbered street in Muenster. The Warm Beer and Bread Bar was five doors up on the right.

Parked out front was a black Ford F150.

Ginger pulled up to a damned meter and found four quarters, enough for an hour.

The Warm Beer was one of Jared Roulan's hangouts, and he'd checked it out the day before, sat at the quiet bar with a Hawkeyes cap pulled low to shade his eyes, ordered a draft and watched the bartender pocket his money, bypassing the register. The girl waiting tables was doing the same thing. At the rate they were ripping off the owner, he was surprised the place was still open.

Ginger, a man of principles despite his profession, had wanted to grab the long-haired asshole by the collar and turn him upside down, shake all the stolen change out of his pockets. Then grab the girl and give her the same treatment.

But he remembered Hitman Rule Number Ten: Don't stand out. Blend in.

So he sat there and drank his beer and watched the employees skim the profits.

Today the jukebox throbbed with country music. At the end of the bar, holding court on a leather-covered stool, was a brash young man with blond hair, brushed back, with a swatch that defied combing and drooped over his forehead. At least ten men and women of a similar age surrounded him, laughing, fawning over whatever it was he was dishing out.

Jared Roulan and *his* posse. They were applauding him, clapping him on the back, wishing him well at his trial.

Ginger watched him reach behind a curvy redhead, squeeze her shapely ass. A brunette leaned down and kissed him on the lips. Star fuckers, groupies, hungry for a piece of whatever was hot at the moment. The guys were just as bad. Fist-bumping, thigh-slapping, half-drunk, they roared at his jokes.

"What'll it be, sweetie?" the server asked.

"Bud Light."

Nobody remembered a guy who ordered a Bud Light.

He sipped his beer and left as silently as he had come.

* * *

Ginger's off-brand motel room was tiny. He would have preferred a Holiday Inn, but the next one was two counties over.
He threw himself onto the bed and drifted off.

All his adult life, Ginger Gallagher had awakened each day at five. By five forty-five the next morning, he had showered and stopped by Joe, Muenster's one coffee shop, for a cup of dark roast to go.

The Roulan ranch was fifteen minutes away. Ginger turned up the drive. If a camera picked up his license number—and it probably would—the Hyundai was a rental, arranged by Paladin in the name of a corporate megafarm operation in Idaho that didn't actually exist.

Half a mile down the single-lane dirt road, bordered on both sides by Iowa corn, Ginger saw the house, a seven-column monstrosity that shouted money. Three large barns sat behind it, and he saw pastures and cows, some eating grass, some lined up at a massive watering trough.

Pulling out his binoculars, he trained them on the field. There was the playboy, possibly a little hungover, blond hair in his eyes, pushing bales of hay off the back of his pickup, like an assembly line, bale after bale. Cattle wandered over, thankful for a chance to rip off a nice hay breakfast.

Ginger had done his homework. The Roulans fed their cows twice a day, and Jared was one of the feeders. Second sitting would be in seven hours, at two in the afternoon.

He backed out, didn't believe the boy had noticed his vehicle.
Today was the day Jamie Muenster was supposed to die.

Muenster Implement carried tractors, trailers, combines and cultivators. Powerful equipment that demanded extreme caution when using. Lots of people died on those machines. Ginger had looked it up. In agribusiness, accidents were the number one cause of death.

He was in the parking lot before the showroom opened, along with three pickups, customers wanting an early start on their day.

At seven-thirty, Cowboy dropped Jamie off. Ginger watched him—dressed today in pressed jeans and a collared, checkered shirt—unlock the door. One by one, employees entered. Five of them by seven forty-five.

The lot was loaded with equipment, both new and used. A few customers wandered among the green John Deeres and red New Hollands. A couple of worn yellow Allis-Chalmer combines kept each other company by the fence.

Anything could happen on one those behemoths. It could flip over, someone could fall off—or, worse, get caught up in the machinery. You never knew.

A fall from a combine, a blow to the head. Accidents happened. He could come back at closing time. The mayor would still be around, an accident could be arranged.

The café was busy at noon.

Hitman Rule Number Seven: Don't become a regular.

But two times didn't make him a regular, and the Paradise cheeseburger was *really* good. Soft bun, grilled to perfection.

Ginger sat in a booth, back to the wall, studying his phone, one eye on the door and the customers. Jared Roulan came in at twelve-thirty. Three studs with him. Tough guys. The customers quieted down for a moment, all eyes watching the blond superstar and his companions.

A town of three hundred needed its celebrities, and Jared was at the top of Muenster's list. It would be rude to ask for the autograph of a possible rapist and murderer, but the customers looked almost ready to take that chance.

Ginger Gallagher observed it all. Feeding time at Roulan's ranch was at two. Closing time at Muenster Implement was at six. He sipped his coffee and bit into his burger. Pickle, mustard —just the right mix. Damn, a perfect meal.

Back at Roulan's ranch, Ginger parked just off the main road and raised his binoculars. There was Jared, with a truck bed full of corn or wheat or whatever the hell cows eat.

Eliminate the eyewitness. That was the mission Ginger had accepted. With Jamie Muenster out of the way, the case against Jared Roulan, the son of a bitch, would have to be dismissed.

But last night in his room, he'd looked it up online. Eliminate the *defendant*, and the case would also be dismissed.

He walked down the lane, carrying a hefty oak branch he'd found in a ditch by the road. If anyone stopped him, he'd be a representative of a megafarm conglomerate, checking the lay of the land. Any interest in selling your ranch, sir?

Jared Roulan didn't hear him until it was too late. Ginger put muscle into the swing, and the branch connected with Roulan's head with a satisfying *thwack*. The boy crumpled and lay still. Approaching the cattle clustered near the feed truck, Ginger pulled his Glock and fired two shots, then took off running.

Back at the road, he trained his binoculars on the stampede his gunfire had caused. Maybe thirty cows trampled the body lying sprawled on the ground.

Here's another fun ag fact, Ginger thought. *Cows kill more people than bears, mountain lions, poisonous snakes, even sharks, though sharks get most of the glory.*

"Death by shark" makes a much better headline than "death by cow."

Three hours later, many miles from Muenster at a little place called the Select Grill, Ginger's phone rang.

"Paladin?"

"Yeah. You take care of business there yet?"

"Getting ready."

He studied the calendar hanging by the register. A group of black and white cows stared out at him. The caption read, "A stampede at the dairy farm resulted in udder chaos." Ginger shook his head.

"Never mind," Paladin said. "Suspect died in a freak accident, and the case against him's been dismissed, so the client's called off the hit."

"Message received."

There was a pause. "Did you have anything to do with—"

"Me? No, I needed a payday as much as—"

"You can keep the down payment. That was part of the deal."

Ginger nodded.

"Crush the phone," Paladin said. "Get in touch when you're ready for your next assignment."

Ginger hung up and took a bite of his burger. The bun was a little stale, the burger not grilled quite the way he liked it. Not nearly as good as the cheeseburger at the Paradise Café, but there were times when you had to make do.

There were ten Hitman Rules, but Ginger Gallagher had invented an eleventh:

A job's a job, but sometimes you have to do what you think is right.

Volcano
Released 1979

"Fins"
"Volcano"
"Treat Her Like a Lady"
"Stranded on a Sandbar"
"Chansons Pour Les Petits Enfants"
"Survive"
"Lady I Can't Explain"
"Boat Drinks"
"Dreamsicle"
"Sending the Old Man Home"
"Woman of Heart and Mind"
"Judgment of the Moon and Stars (Ludwig's Tune)"

All songs by Jimmy Buffett,
except "Fins" (with Deborah McColl,
Barry Chance, and Tom Corcoran),
"Volcano" (with Keith Sykes and Harry Dailey),
"Treat Her Like a Lady" (with David Loggins),
and "Survive" (with Mike Utley).

VOLCANO

Alison McMahan

When the phone rang, all three of Keith's managers and both of his agents were on the line. Keith was already in New York, they said, prepping the play, and the play needed help, so would I get on the next plane east?

I dicked them around a bit, which got me all-expenses-paid instead of most-expenses-paid, along with a hefty paycheck. But there was never any question in my mind. I was packing for October in New York with one hand, even as I played hard to get on the phone.

And now here I was, in the fabulous Broadhigh Theater.

"The play" was based on my screenplay for the movie that had elevated Keith into superstardom thirty years ago. The movie that had turned Keith into Smokey Rob for life.

Just looking at the set, I could tell the play was taking a lot of liberties with my original script. I could see the vista of Three Mile Island through the set window, sure, but not much else matched.

"What're you doing with a machete? It's supposed to be a boomerang," I said to Keith's still-impossibly-broad back. "And where's the picture of the Ayatollah?"

He swiveled around. "Oh, thank god you're here. I need help. As you can see." He sliced the air with the machete. His biceps were as round and his legs as shapely as ever.

I'd been angry with him for thirty years, but now that I was in a room with him, he still made my knees tremble and my belly flutter.

I swallowed and made my way up onto the stage.

Close up, I could see what the airbrushing and the makeup and the good cinematography concealed: the crow's feet around his eyes, the gray roots in his dyed black hair. His cheekbones, once pronounced and haughty, were now round and pink, like Santa Claus. Was the cute little Cuban hat he wore hiding a bald spot?

"I dunno why I ever let them talk me into this," he said, swinging the machete with the same glorious aplomb of his Uzi-wielding movie days. "There's just no way to show the best action moments in a theater."

"I know, right?" I tried to sound just as surprised by this as he was. "Pretty tough to make a cheery musical out of an action film with a high body count." I didn't mention that I knew the play had been his idea. Better to get right to how I was going to earn the paycheck. "So, Keith, why am I here?"

He got down on one knee. "I need you. I need you to save me. Save all this."

And that was it. No *I'm sorry I dumped you.* No *I'm sorry I got rich and left you to a lifetime of service jobs and poorly paying gigs.* Not even a *Long time no see.*

Nope. All that mattered was that I save his hide. Take the mess they'd made of my screenplay and rewrite it. Make it truer to my original vision. The vision Keith had abandoned as soon as money and fame beckoned, the same way he'd abandoned our vision of us as the Schwarzenegger/Shriver of the indie movie world.

I chewed my lip in silence, my thirty-year-old anger duking it out with my desire to make things right. To reclaim what I had created.

To earn that check.

And to deal with my reawakened attraction to him.

"You want me to beg, I'll beg," said Keith. "You brought the magic then. I need you to bring it back now. Otherwise, that's it for me. I'll be finished, a has-been."

Over the years, I'd fantasized about this moment. A lot. In my version of this scene, he'd also invited me back into his bed. Back to the passenger seat of his glamorous life with its huge carbon footprint.

As if.

But no, no romps in the dressing room. I was there to fix the play.

A difficult job, to say the least, involving a lot of late nights, a lot of tearing of hair and grinding of teeth. Think of a surgeon on his feet for forty-eight straight hours doing emergency procedures and you'll have the idea—except to me it felt more like forty-eight *weeks*. I rewrote throughout rehearsals, through all the previews, and through the opening month. You could come to the show every night during that period and see almost a completely different play.

The cast hated me, hated each day's new pages. New pages meant learning new lines, new blocking, even new set and costume changes. Keith got so testy the producer instructed me to avoid him backstage; like most movie stars, he wasn't all that great at learning lines, and the producer feared he would fire me in a fit of pique.

The producer also confided that Keith was broke. Too many lawsuits, the result of his vicious temper. Too many ex-wives, for the same reason.

It was up to me to save him.

So I rewrote until our initial run was locked in, and then I rewrote some more until I was sure the run would be extended, and then some more after that until the play was nominated for a Tony.

The only times I saw Keith were at the obligatory crew parties at the mandated water hole for the benefit of the paparazzi. We were only really *alone*, if you can call it that, when the press interviewed us together. Then we'd sit cozily on a loveseat, facing bloggers who made a big deal of the magic Keith and I had made in the past.

When they asked why we'd stopped working together, I jumped in and lied through my teeth: "We never stopped. We've developed all sorts of projects. But we had to wait for the right moment and the right backers, backers with vision."

I didn't realize how much the idea that we'd been secretly developing some brilliant project had taken hold in Keith's mind until I found him waiting for me at the stage door after the show one night.

"Here, let me get that for you." He took the bigger of my two messenger bags, the one filled with drafts, notebooks, and my laptop. It looked minuscule in his hand.

When he reached for the other bag, I twisted away.

The hotel was a short walk from the theater, but Keith hailed a cab. I thought it was because he didn't want to be out in the freezing cold. Imagine my surprise when he told the driver to take us to the executive airport in Westchester.

"Wait, what?" I watched the turn for my hotel and its welcoming bathtub whiz by. "You're not firing me, are you?"

"Why would I do that?" Keith sounded genuinely aggrieved. "I thought you could use some time off. Thought I'd take you on a little vacation." He opened my messenger bag, unzipped the inside pocket, and pulled out my passport. "Ah, I see you still carry your passport wherever you go. Excellent!" He flipped it open.

"Give me that."

He handed it over with a laugh. "You look much better in person."

That almost sounded like flirting. I felt my resolve begin to crumble. "Where are we going?"

"You'll see."

* * *

Our plane was a Hawker 900XP executive jet, white with blue accents. There was a female captain and a male co-pilot named Raleigh, who served us our dinner en route. He was so young and handsome that I almost forgot I'd been carrying a torch for Keith my whole life. I made a clumsy attempt to engage him in conversation. "So, you been flying with Keith long?"

"Oh, yeah," he said. "I've been through all the crashes with him. He says I'm his good luck charm. He won't fly without me."

"The crashes?" All lustful thoughts went right out of my head. "In, uhm, this plane?"

"This plane can fly through anything. One time in the Yukon, I thought we were going to smack right into a glacier."

"That time in Mexico was worse," muttered Keith. "You definitely don't want to crash-land in Mexico."

"Buzzard's Bay was the worst." Raleigh topped off my drink. "But Smokey Rob always saves us." He winked at me, cleared our dishes, then pulled down the rear seats to make them into two beds.

"Better catch some shut-eye," Keith said.

"How can I sleep if I don't even know where we're going?"

I'd finished my wine, and now Keith handed me a brandy. "Have you ever seen a live volcano?"

I froze, the glass halfway to my mouth. "Say what?"

"It's one of the calmer ones. Strombolian."

As if I was supposed to know what that meant.

"It's been sort of *burping* every twenty minutes for the last two hundred years. I thought it would be cool to see it."

"Burping? What do you mean *burping*?" I drew my second bag a little closer.

"It's completely safe." Keith drained his glass and pressed a button. The cabin lights dimmed.

He was asleep almost instantly, leaving me to wonder what he was up to. Obviously not seduction.

I undid the clasp of the bag I hadn't let him take, pulled out my nose tubes and put them on. The benefit of being a writer is that no one looks at you. No one had noticed my breathing issues, or that my messenger bag contained an oxygen concentrator. Up to now, I'd managed to get through the long days of rehearsal and the long nights of performance by retreating to my private dressing room—one of the perks I'd negotiated—at regular intervals and sucking in oxygen.

Being kidnapped and taken to visit a volcano somewhere in the Caribbean might *sound* romantic, but it's less fun if you have to live in the clothes you slept in throughout the trip.

As the sun rose, we descended onto the island's grass airstrip. The handsome co-pilot headed off for the makeshift hangar with our passports as I stumbled down the plane's airstair, the pressure around my ribs loosening a smidge with the humidity.

A man stood by a jeep. Very young, with a broad forehead framed perfectly by an even crown of tight black curls. He was so thin that, when he smiled at us, his eyes and cheeks crinkled, making him look older than he was.

He hopped into the driver's seat. Keith got in beside him, and I slid into the back, where I could sneak sips of oxygen if I needed them.

The volcano lay dead ahead. It looked so close, I was sure we would reach it quickly and said so to our guide—who'd introduced himself as Hilberto. "No, it's farther off than it looks."

We bumped along a dirt road. Women and little children peered at us from the jungle on either side. The kids chased the jeep, screaming and laughing. We saw no other vehicles.

"Not a lot of tourists come here, Hilberto?"

He raised a hand from the wheel and struck his chest. "Only the chief's family can go up the volcano. I am the chief's son." The jeep swerved, and he grabbed the wheel with both hands. "This is my job, to take people to the top and bring them down again. Best job on the island."

"You see?" Keith had turned around and directed this at me. In his floppy straw hat and reflective sunglasses, his cheeks and nose white with zinc oxide, he looked more like someone's elderly aunt than a movie star.

"See what?"

He started to answer, then waved the question away. "Just wait."

I felt like I was missing something. See *what*? The dense jungle around us held no answers.

I hadn't slept much on the plane, and the rough ride made me carsick. I gripped the back of Keith's seat and closed my eyes.

Suddenly we emerged from shade into bright sunlight. I opened my eyes, and there it was, the volcano, a wisp of white smoke rising lazily from its top. It was a huge mountain with gently sloping sides, surrounded by ash fields. We skimmed along the top of the ash layer, almost like a motorboat on water.

The volcano was imposing, regal. It demanded respect. It made more sense now that only a chief and his family were allowed close to it.

The further Hilberto drove across the lunar landscape of the ash field, the more I felt myself on the flank of something alive and breathing.

As we climbed the mountain, the air became drier and thinner, and the pressure around my ribs got tighter and tighter.

At last we stopped.

"Now we walk," said Hilberto. He got out of the car and started up the steep slope.

Keith noticed the oxygen concentrator's case slung across my chest. "Why don't you leave your bag in the jeep? No one's going to take it."

"It's fine," I snapped.

He shrugged. "Suit yourself." He started up the steep hillside. I straggled behind, gasping.

At last we reached the top. Hilberto stood on the rim, looking down into the crater at a seething magma lake.

There is no describing that sight. A magma lake is earth's answer to the sun.

The only correct response was to get down on my knees. I wanted to absorb the force of it, not just through my eyes, but through my joints, to feel the warmth of the ash rise through my legs and arms and heal my heart.

I reached out with one hand, then another, as the volcano heaved up a huge cloud of dust and smoke.

I turned to Keith, my mouth wide with awe. "Thank you for bringing me here."

Keith tossed his floppy hat into the volcano's mouth.

"No!" cried Hilberto. "You must show the volcano respect!"

We watched the hat float down lazily, spiraling as it caught some invisible air current, finally hitting the magma far below us. It sat on the surface of the lava lake, apparently unharmed, for a brief moment. I guess I've seen too many volcano movies, because I expected it to burst into flame.

Instead, it—well, it just *melted*.

"Do you have a camera?"

I pulled out my cell phone. "Only this."

Keith nodded. "Good enough." He took off his sunglasses, wiped the zinc oxide from his nose and cheeks, assumed his famous expression—and there he was, Smokey Rob, in the flesh.

I started recording video.

"Just picture it," Keith declaimed. "The hero struggles with the bad guys on the lip of the volcano." He mimed a fight scene. Jab. Cross. Slip sideways to evade an enemy. A series of quick knee strikes, holding the imaginary bad guy's head down so that he'd get the knee full in the face. Punch to the liver. And then his signature move, a right overhand strike to the temple.

"The volcano erupts," he went on. "But the bad guys don't quit. They struggle with our hero on the edge! Who will win?"

This was Keith's gift. Once he went into his Smokey Rob character, you forgot he was ever anyone else.

I kept the video running. I now realized what he was up to: this was the pitch we would show producers. The incredible location, the incredible star. Aging, maybe, but he still had it.

"Smokey Rob. You are *Smokey Rob!*" Hilberto cried.

I let the phone drop.

"Keep filming," Keith ordered, and then, to Hilberto: "Yes, I am Smokey Rob."

Hilberto was beside himself. He jumped around, fists up, as if he were ready to box. "I must fight you! Fight! Fight!"

Keith smiled. "I'll make sure you get a part in the movie, Hilberto. Maybe we can have a fight scene."

I was feeling a bit nauseated. I assumed it was the altitude. And there was a stink like rotten eggs in the air.

But Hilberto wouldn't give up. "We must fight! I will defeat Smokey Rob and become the next chief of my village!"

I went up to Hilberto and put a hand on his arm. "Hilberto, Keith is an old man now. He doesn't really fight. His fights are staged for the movies. You understand?"

"I understand movies, yes. We have VHS. *Smokey Rob Shoots First. Smokey Rob Shoots First and Second. Smokey Rob Kills Them All.*"

I winced at the titles of the horrible sequels Keith had made after dumping me.

"It's okay," said Keith. "He wants to fight me, I'll fight. I never say no to a fan."

Then he leaned closer and whispered: "I'm not *that* old, you know. I still got it."

So he still cared what I thought of him.

"Don't worry, I still lava you," I whispered back, grinning.

For a moment I thought he might kiss me.

But then Hilberto sucker-punched him, a cross right to the gut. Keith gasped, his mouth pursing like a fish out of water.

"Hilberto, wait until I tell you to start!" I waved my phone. "You want the chief to see you fight, don't you?"

But Hilberto was a man on a mission. He delivered an upper

cut to Keith's solar plexus.

Keith was angry now, I could tell. I saw him wind up for the overhand. I'd seen him do this move many times—in practice, in boxing matches, on film. A few of those times, people had gotten hurt.

"No! Keith, don't!"

Too late. Keith's fist met Hilberto's temple.

And Hilberto went down.

Keith doubled over, trying to get his wind back.

I knelt next to Hilberto. There was a long fissure next to where he had fallen, and the rotten egg smell was coming from there, stronger now.

A caterpillar of fear wiggled around in my chest.

Please, Hilberto, don't be dead.

I rolled him onto his side. There was blood on the back of his head.

The lunar-like surface made everything look smooth, but Hilberto's head had hit a rock buried under the layer of ash.

"Help me get him down to the jeep."

Smoke spewed from the volcano. Thick billowing smoke, not the wispy white stuff we'd seen earlier. So much of it that the day darkened perceptibly.

I reached into my messenger bag and inserted the canula into my nose.

"What the hell is that?"

I tried to act nonchalant. "Portable oxygen tank. I have COPD. You'll have to carry him. Come on, let's go."

"I didn't know you were sick." Keith said. "You should have told me."

"I was afraid you wouldn't hire me if you knew. And I needed the money. Desperately."

But Keith wasn't listening. He bent down and put two fingers to Hilberto's neck, then looked up, his face ashen. "He's dead."

"No!" I dropped to my knees and started CPR.

But it was no use. Hilberto was gone.

Keith pulled me up. "We have to get out of here."

"We still have to take him down." I grabbed Hilberto's feet.

"Come on. I'll help. Grab his arms."

But Keith did indeed still have it. He hoisted Hilberto, cradling him lovingly, as if the young man were a child.

Instead of heading down the mountain, though, he went up. Back to the lip of the volcano.

"No!" I screamed.

But Keith dropped the body over the edge.

Now Hilberto's family would never see him again, never know what happened. It would be as if Hilberto, son of an island chief, had never walked the earth.

"Why did you do that?" I demanded.

"He was already dead. What difference does it make?"

"But—"

"No one would believe he went crazy and attacked us. No one would believe I hit him in self-defense. Now we can say he jumped. Or whatever you come up with."

I stared at him. "Whatever *I* come up with? I had nothing to do with it. This is all on you, Keith."

"Come on, honey. We gotta present a united front on this. So we can do our next project. It'll be just like old times."

And of course, the volcano chose that moment to blow.

First came the lightning, flashing from the ground up.

Then a huge belch of rocks, dust, smoke, and magma. A shower of hot pebbles rained down on us.

Keith gripped my arm. "We gotta go."

"I'm not going anywhere with you." I tried to pull away.

"Don't be stupid. We have to get off this island."

I could see magma oozing slowly from the gas vent that had gotten to Hilberto, right behind Keith.

"I loved you so much," I said.

"I still love you." Keith pulled me close and kissed me, oxygen tube and all, one of those cinematic kisses that make your toes curl. The kiss I'd spent my adult life longing for.

All of those years of longing, wasted.

I put my hands on his chest and pushed.

Hard.

He stumbled. Just a little stumble, but that's all it took. He stepped right into the lava.

He looked down at his feet, a puzzled look on his face. Then he looked at me. Reached for me, the same begging look on his face that I'd never been able to refuse.

Until now.

Maybe I could have saved him. I don't know. The lava around him was already turning dark, but the place he'd stepped in was bright red. His jeans burst into flame.

I could hear him screaming as I hobbled down to the jeep.

The best thing I ever wrote was the eulogy I gave at Keith's memorial service in the meadow behind his ranch at Comanche Sky Park. I described his last moments, how brave he was, carrying me to safety, then rushing back up the mountain in a vain attempt to save poor Hilberto.

This was, of course, an audition, and it was a successful one. Before the last rose was dropped over the empty coffin by the army of female fans that had managed to infiltrate the service, one of Keith's agents pulled me aside and asked for a meeting to discuss a movie deal based on Keith's exploits on the volcano.

So as things turned out, I've given Keith everything he wanted. He's a hero again. There he stands on the screen, larger than life, played by a body builder destined to be the Next Big Action Star. This new Keith has the original's doe eyes and a sad look that arouses tenderness in women. Watch him vault over the lava flow to save me, his old love, still his true love, in glorious 3D on the IMAX screen.

I have so many job offers now, I think I'll buy Keith's plane.

And hire Raleigh to fly it.

Coconut Telegraph
Released 1981

"Coconut Telegraph"
"Incommunicado"
"It's My Job"
"Growing Older But Not Up"
"The Good Fight"
"The Weather is Here, Wish You Were Beautiful"
"Stars Fell on Alabama"
"Island"
"Little Miss Magic"

All songs by Jimmy Buffett,
except "Incommunicado" (with Deborah McColl and M.L. Benoit),
"It's My Job" (by Mac McAnally), "The Good Fight" (with J.D. Souther),
"Stars Fell on Alabama" (by Mitchell Parish and Frank Perkins),
and "Island" (with David Loggins).

INCOMMUNICADO

Bruce Robert Coffin

Jake had been trudging along on the burning asphalt for the better part of three hours when the Cadillac first came into view. He thought the soles of his boots were melting, and a blister was forming on his right foot. Having polished off the only water he carried more than an hour before, his mouth was too dry to spit. He'd figured that someone traveling along the godforsaken Arizona two-lane would have picked him up long before now, but he'd figured wrong. He really needed this ride.

As it drew nearer, the Caddy's aqua blue lacquer and chrome shimmered in the heat waves rising from the pavement. Jake adjusted the straps on his knapsack, painted on his most disarming smile, and stuck out a thumb.

The ragtop rolled to a stop beside him. Its only occupant was a paunchy middle-aged man with a cleft chin and a wispy gray mustache. He wore a tan Stetson, cargo shorts, and an obnoxiously loud Hawaiian shirt covered in red and green parrots. A pair of reflective sunglasses and an open bottle of Dos Equis balanced on the seat between his legs completed this rolling mid-life crisis.

If there was one thing prison had taught Jake, it was how to select a mark, and the oaf seated behind the wheel of the Caddy fit the bill nicely.

"Howdy, amigo," the driver said, his words basted in a

southern drawl as thick as chicken gravy. "Where ya headed?"

"Anywhere but here," Jake croaked, his eyes settling on the large diamond-and-gold ring adorning one of the man's fingers.

"Hop in," the driver said. "Toss your load in the back."

Happy to be rid of his burden, Jake dropped his satchel onto the rear seat beside a large plastic cooler, then reached for the door handle, his smile widening. His ship, as they say, had finally come in.

Jake plopped down onto a mile of ivory-colored cowhide as his host thrust out a meaty paw. "Friends call me the Duke."

Resisting the urge to roll his eyes at the lame nickname, Jake played along. "As in John Wayne?"

"You're darn tootin', Pilgrim," the Duke said, drawing out the words in a mediocre imitation of Marion Michael Morrison. "What can I say? I'm a fan."

"Nice to meet you, Duke," Jake said, gripping the clammy offering while eyeing the shiny ring again and wondering how much he might be able to get for it.

"You must be parched," the Duke said, cocking a thumb over his shoulder. "Help yourself to a cold one. Might as well grab me a fresh one, too."

Jake reached into the back and pulled two ice-cold bottles from the cooler. He handed one to the Duke, then twisted the cap off his own and drank. It was heavenly. He took another long swig, relishing the feel of the carbonation soothing his dry throat, his mind racing for an answer to what would undoubtedly be the Duke's next question.

"What do they call *you*?" the Duke asked, sure enough.

"Travis," Jake said, appropriating the name from the dog-eared John D. MacDonald paperback stuffed inside his knapsack. "Travis McGee."

"Welcome aboard, Mr. McGee."

And, just like that, they were on their way.

* * *

The Duke kept the needle pegged at a constant ninety miles an hour. The Caddy's engine purred without a hitch. Traffic, as it had been during Jake's three-hour trek, was nonexistent.

"Nice ride," Jake said.

The Duke's face beamed with pride. "This here's a '59 Eldorado Biarritz. My baby. They only produced about thirteen hundred of these, you know. Biggest tail fins ever."

Jake pointed at the speedometer. "Aren't you worried about getting pulled over?"

"Out here?" the Duke said. "Unlikely. But worry not, *patrón*, on the off chance we do run across the *policia*, I can talk my way out of most anything."

Jake eyed the diamond ring again and wondered how much talking, or begging, the Duke would do when Jake relieved him of his valuables.

As the miles blurred past and morning melted into afternoon, the merciless desert sun continued to beat down upon them. The Duke did most of the talking, droning on about ex-wives and his half dozen or so kids. "And those are just the ones I know about," he said with a snort.

Jake smiled and nodded, but quickly found himself bored. He wondered how much more of this he could stand before making his play.

"You got family?" the Duke asked, finally giving Jake the opportunity to get a word in.

"No one I stay in touch with," Jake said.

"You travel incommunicado, huh?"

"You might say I have fallen out of favor."

The Duke turned his head, appraising Jake, but said nothing.

"So, where are *you* headed?" Jake asked, hoping to acquire some information he could use.

"The Sunshine State. Cedar Key. Ever hear of it?"

"Nope. Vacation?"

"Change of scenery," the Duke said. "I figure a new venue will be better for business."

"What exactly *is* your business?"

The Duke fixed him with a sideways grin. "I'm what you might call a collector."

"Antiques?"

"Sometimes."

"Valuable stuff?"

"Son, the things I collect are priceless." He cocked his thumb toward the back again. "In fact, I got a trunkful."

Wondering what kind of moron picked up strangers while riding around with valuables in the trunk of his classic car, Jake began to fantasize about more than just robbing this bloviating windbag. After all, it was easy to get lost in the middle of nowhere. He was pondering another question about the Duke's priceless collectibles when a roadside eatery appeared in the distance. Its gaudy metal sign rose high above the desert floor like a monument, multicolored neon lights, announcing "Red River BBQ, Best in the State."

Jake scanned the horizon for any hint of flowing water amidst a forest of saguaros. Finding none, he decided the sign must be someone's poor attempt at irony.

"You hungry?" the Duke asked, pulling on the Caddy's reins.

Jake hadn't realized just how famished he was until that very moment. "Yeah, I could eat," he said. He patted his pockets. "Little light on the resources, though."

The Duke placed a hand on Jake's shoulder. "Not to worry, my friend. You're a guest. My treat."

Struggling with an urge to forcibly remove the Duke's hand before bouncing his head off the steering wheel, Jake simply smiled and said, "Thanks."

The Duke angled his gleaming Detroit mount off the blacktop and onto a dusty hard pan where a half dozen pickups, sedans, minivans, and an ugly chartreuse wood-paneled station wagon were parked. The setting was surreal, and Jake half expected to see a surfboard tethered to the roof of the wagon.

The two men climbed out of the car and strode toward the

eatery. Jake was a bit surprised by the Duke's height. At six feet, Jake was no slouch, but the Duke had him by at least six inches. Behind the wheel, he hadn't seemed so tall.

None of the patrons paid them any mind as they entered the air-conditioned restaurant and slid into an empty booth in the far corner. They ordered beer and food. The Duke devoured a rack of ribs, half a chicken, a pulled pork sandwich with fries, and a heaping bowl of coleslaw.

Jake, who hadn't ordered anywhere near that much food, was watching his host glut himself when the idea came to him. He would pretend stomach trouble, and that would give him the opportunity to rob the Duke.

They hadn't been back on the road for long before Jake's stomach really did begin to bother him. That tamale relish might have been a mistake.

"You mind pulling off the road for a sec?" he asked, rubbing his midsection. "My stomach feels a little off."

"Ha," the Duke cackled. "That good southern barbeque too much for ya?"

"Evidently," Jake said. "You mind?"

At the first turnout they came to, the Duke jerked the wheel hard, barely slowing as they rocketed off the highway and deep into scrubland and cacti. Jake glanced back into the rear seat to make sure his knapsack was still there and observed the dust billowing out behind them like a chestnut-colored contrail.

They'd traveled close to a mile from the main road when Jake finally spoke up. "This is probably far enough."

"Don't want you to put your family jewels on display for our fellow travelers," the Duke cracked. With that, he brought the convertible to a sliding stop on the dirt road.

Dust floated around them like smoke. Jake opened his door and gestured toward the trunk. "Don't suppose you've got any T-P in there, do you?"

"Son, I've got all manner of things in there," the Duke said, stepping out of the Cadillac.

Jake waited until the Duke was hunched over the trunk before sliding his switchblade from the pocket of his jeans. He pressed the button on the side of the handle, and the blade snicked out.

The Duke popped the trunk lid and stepped back, and Jake took a look. He half expected to see rolls of toilet paper, a pile of crappy Hawaiian shirts, and whatever else comprised this windbag's soon-to-be-ended life. What he *did* see made his skin crawl. The Caddy's trunk was filled with human hearts, a writhing, pumping mass of moving flesh.

"What the—?"

"Told you, son, I'm a collector," the Duke said, eyeing the contents of his trunk with adoration. "Been at this a long while. You like?"

Jake staggered back a few steps, trying to put some distance between himself and the abomination before him.

The Duke grinned and lowered his aviator glasses to the tip of his nose. "You weren't planning to stick me with that little thing, were you?"

Jake couldn't answer. His mouth had turned as arid as the ground upon which they stood. This was the first time he had seen the Duke's eyes, and they were glowing as red as coals. Jake figured his mind must be playing tricks on him. This asshole was no more a threat than any of his previous marks. A couple of well-placed thrusts of the blade, and he would be on his way.

Lowering himself into a crouch and bending slightly at the knees, Jake adjusted his grip on the switchblade's handle and prepared to carve himself some road turkey. As he lunged toward the Duke, a white-hot pain exploded from his knife hand, surging up his forearm to the elbow. Jake looked down to see a large rattlesnake locked onto his wrist, its mouth stretched wide, its fangs buried in his flesh. He screamed and dropped the weapon. The rattler's eyes bulged, rivulets of blood trickling from its jaws. Jake shook his arm wildly, but the serpent remained locked on like a vise.

"Perhaps I can help," the Duke said, picking up the switchblade.

Jake turned to run, but the ground had turned to quicksand, trapping him. He felt the Duke's hands on his shoulders, his breath hot and rancid beside Jake's face.

"Who are you?" Jake screamed, as the sharp point of the knife entered his torso.

"I think you know, Jacob," the Duke said.

Those were the last words Jake ever heard.

The young woman in denim cutoffs and a low-cut tee strolled along the breakdown lane without a care in the world. She was humming a tune, mildly buzzed, daydreaming about steel drums and rum, when the sleek silver convertible came into view. She adjusted her fanny pack, taking comfort in the heft of the Smith & Wesson .38 Special tucked inside. She stopped walking and struck a pose, thrusting out a thumb and one shapely leg. The two-seater pulled up beside her.

The handsome young man at the wheel wore reflective sunglasses, a Hawaiian shirt covered in red and green parrots, and an expensive Rolex. He was deeply tanned, with a head of thick wavy blond hair.

"Awesome car," the woman said, leaning in to display a bit more cleavage and get a closer look at his watch.

The driver grinned. "My baby. '55 Porsche 550 Spyder. I call it Little Bastard."

The woman laughed. "Looks like one *fast* little bastard."

"It is," he said. "Where are you headed?"

"Me? I never really plan that far ahead."

"Well, you're more than welcome to join me. I'm headed for a place just east of Eden."

"Sounds like fun," she said, thinking, *After I relieve you of your watch and wallet.*

The driver offered her his hand. "Name's Jim."

They shook, and she offered him a lie: "I'm Julie."

"Julie," Jim repeated, his grin widening into a flawless smile. "Hop in, darlin'."

Somewhere Over China
Released 1982

"Where's the Party"
"It's Midnight and I'm Not Famous Yet"
"I Heard I Was in Town"
"Somewhere Over China"
"When Salome Plays the Drum"
"Lip Service"
"If I Could Just Get it on Paper"
"Steamer"
"On a Slow Boat to China"

All songs by Jimmy Buffett,
except "Where's the Party" (with Steve Goodman and Bill LaBounty),
"It's Midnight and I'm Not Famous Yet" (with Steve Goodman),
"I Heard I Was in Town" and "Lip Service" (both with Michael Utley),
"Steamer" (by John Scott Sherrill),
and "On a Slow Boat to China" (by Frank Loesser).

IF I COULD JUST GET IT ON PAPER

Lissa Marie Redmond

Dan held the door open for Shanna, whose eyes squinted against the inky darkness of the bar after the dazzling sunlight of the afternoon. "Welcome to the Strange Bird," he said.

Tucking her cell phone into the back pocket of her jeans, she looked around. Now that her eyes were accustomed to the lighting, she could see the torn fishing nets and old rusted rods and reels hanging from the walls. The ceiling was covered in stapled dollar bills with black Sharpie messages scribbled on them: *Brett's Stag 2017. Carol and Walter. Buffalo Wyoming '08.*

"We call the décor Old Key West Local. The tourists like to come here from Duval Street so they can say they experienced an authentic Key West bar."

"What about him?" Shanna gestured to the man passed out face down on the bar near the corner.

"That's Billy the Squid. Every dive bar needs its local lush. We leave him be. Makes the tourists think they're drinking with Ernest Hemingway," he laughed, ushering her farther into the establishment.

"Was Hemingway ever here?"

"This place was built in 1971, so no. But don't tell the customers that." Dan lifted the rail and slid behind the scratched and scarred wooden bar. "I just say we've been around as long

113

as I've been in Key West—which is true, since I came down from Cleveland in 1994."

Shanna had just moved from Iowa herself. Forty-two and freshly divorced, she had finally taken the advice of her ex-sister-in-law: "Get out of this state, get away from my brother, and start a new life while you still look good." Not very empowering, even when she first heard it fifteen years ago at her stagette party, but when her aunt offered her a room in her bungalow until she could get back on her feet, Shanna had jumped on it.

"Your Aunt Sarah's good people," Dan said. "She knows how busy we get Super Bowl weekend and I'm short a bartender. She said you worked in a busy place back home?"

"The VFW in Bryden Lake, Iowa. It was the only place to drink in our otherwise dry county."

Dan nodded and arranged some glasses. "I know it's short notice, but I can't have just two people manning the bar on the busiest night of the year."

The Squid snorted from his perch and turned his face toward the wall.

Shanna smiled, showing off a set of straight white teeth. "We're interrupting his slumber."

"Nah. The place could be on fire, and he'd be oblivious. Don't worry about the Squid; he's harmless."

A banging on the front door turned their attention from the snoring man. Dan unlocked it to admit a tired fisherman type. "Sorry, Dan," he said. "I just got Carl Needham's money. I hope you didn't give our square away."

"Anyone else but you, I would have." Dan was all business now. "Abel, this is Shanna, our new bartender. She's Sarah Boyington's niece. She's going to be working for me, starting today."

"Super Bowl Sunday? Have a heart, Dan. The poor lady's going to run her feet off."

"I'm pretty good on my feet, actually." Shanna held out a hand. "Shanna Maxwell."

Abel looked sheepish and wiped his hands on the front of his bib overalls. "I've been fishing since before sunup, Miss. I wouldn't want you to smell like the catch of the day while you're working."

"But you got no problem handing me three thousand dollars in stanky cash?" Dan asked.

The leathery skin around Abel's watery blue eyes crinkled. "Nope. I figure money's money, no matter what the aroma." He pulled a wad of hundreds from his pocket and handed it to Dan, who proceeded to count every bill.

When he was satisfied it was all there, he walked back to a door marked *Office* and disappeared inside, coming out with a gray lockbox. He pulled a chain with a small key dangling from it from inside his golf shirt and over his head. He unlocked the steel box and stashed the money inside. "You're the last person to pay up. Next year, you don't get the money to me on time, your square is gone. I got ten guys on a waitlist as it is."

Abel nodded. "Understandable. I sure could use that hundred and fifty thousand payoff."

"So could everyone who buys a square. Even me." Dan slipped the key back around his neck and put the lockbox on the bar. "I'll see you at five. I got six hundred bucks riding on Cleveland."

"Cleveland?" Abel made his way back to the door, turning the deadbolt with callused fingers. "I hope you got good odds."

Shanna watched Dan lock the box and take it back to the office.

"I run one of the biggest football pools on the Key," he told her. "Three hundred thousand bucks in payoffs. Three thousand a square to buy in."

"You keep three hundred thousand cash in this place?"

Dan shook his head. What was left of his graying brown hair was pulled back into a skinny ponytail, an aging hipster's attempt to draw attention from his receding hairline. "I'm not stupid. Except for Abel's three grand, the rest is in a safe-deposit box at the bank. You'll meet Charlie Mullins in a few minutes. He's a

115

retired Boston cop, and, once a year on Hangover Monday, he straps on his .357 Magnum, and we take a ride to the bank. We bring the cash back here and wait for the winners to show up to collect."

"Aren't football pools illegal in Florida?"

Dan cocked a bushy eyebrow. "This is the Conch Republic, my dear, not *Florida*. Long as we don't make waves, the local authorities ignore us. Right, Squid?"

The Squid raised his head in bleary recognition, then slumped back into unconsciousness.

"Is he okay?"

"He's fine, ain't you, Squid?" Dan maneuvered around the drunk and began to pry him from his stool, caught the poor guy's ratty backpack before it hit the floor. "What do you have in this thing? Bricks?"

"Books," Squid said, his voice groggy. "What time is it?" The man could have been forty or eighty; it was impossible for Shanna to tell. He had mussy blondish hair that hung in his eyes and a pale sunken face. Worn jeans hung on his skinny hips, and his dirty T-shirt read *What Happens in Vegas, Stays in Vegas!*

"Almost noon. Time for you to go take a shower and eat something."

The Squid swayed a little, trying to focus on Shanna. He stuck out a boney hand. "Hello, there. I'm Bill."

"Good to meet you, Bill."

"Billy the Squid," Dan laughed, "our own resident barnacle. Get going now, Squid. We'll see you later."

The Squid's eyes flicked to Dan for a second, then he shuffled to the door.

A huge barrel-chested man pushed past him. "Out of the way, Squid. Dan's got a *paying* customer coming in."

The Squid didn't answer, just set off down the street.

The big man let the door swing closed behind him, then noticed the pretty blonde standing in the middle of the room. "I'm sorry, Miss. I didn't know anyone was here."

"Charlie Mullins, this is Shanna, my new bartender. She's Sarah's niece."

Charlie engulfed her hand in a sweaty shake. "Good to meet you."

Dan grabbed a glass from the rack in front of him and began to polish it. "Charlie's my head of security during football pool season."

Charlie winked at Shanna and slid his bulk onto a stool, his giant belly pressed up against the wood. "How about a pot of coffee before the crowd gets here? You drink coffee, Shawna?"

"Shanna," she corrected him. "Actually, I'm more of a tea person."

"Shanna, my bad. I'm actually more of a whisky person, but I got to be on my game today. Ain't that right, Dan?"

Dan made his way to the coffee machine at the end of the bar. "This is a morning tradition with us. Charlie comes in every day before I open, and we drink coffee. Don't be surprised to see us here some days when you open."

"Or the Squid, either," Charlie threw in.

"You let him sleep here?" Shanna took a stool a couple spots down from Charlie. There was something greasy about the man that made her want to put some space between them.

Dan shrugged. "He showed up here about five years ago, started hanging around the bar. He wasn't as bad then as he is now. One day he let it slip that Billy the Kid was killed in the New Mexico town where he's from. I overheard that and dubbed him Billy the Squid, and it stuck. Poor bastard. Lives behind a T-shirt shop two streets over."

"That's so sad," Shanna said.

Charlie accepted the mug of coffee Dan brought him and took a sip. "Where's the cream and sugar?"

"I only got two hands, you washed-up old fart." Dan retrieved a carton of creamer and a bowl of sugar from behind the counter, and the two of them poured copious amounts of each into their cups.

"Don't feel sorry for the Squid. Me and the other bartenders used to play Rock, Paper, Scissors to see who'd have to carry him home," Dan told her. "We got tired of it after a while, and now we just let him pass out here."

"You should charge him rent." Charlie blew steam from his mug and took another sip. "Ahh, perfect."

Dan leaned across the bar. "Let's get our game plan together for tomorrow. I don't want any of the winners in here until the three hundred grand is locked in the office."

"What do you want me to do?" Shanna asked.

"Come back behind the bar and familiarize yourself with everything. It's going to be a busy night."

The Strange Bird was packed. Half the crowd was wearing brown and orange, the other half was in blue. Friendly taunts were tossed around between plays. For most of the crowd, who won was unimportant. It was the spread that counted.

All the regulars were there. Abel, Carl Needham, and Liam Sullivan sat at their regular table in the corner with the rest of their fishing-boat crew. All the once-in-a-whiles were out in full force as well: Korey White, Bram Washington, Hector Morales. Most importantly, Robert "Bobby" Balzano and his son, Bobby Junior.

The Balzanos had moved down to the Keys from New Jersey after doing a five-year stint in federal prison for racketeering. Being ex-cons didn't seem to impact their lifestyle or cash flow much. Both were partial to black track suits and gaudy gold chains. Both had bottle-blond girlfriends with big hair, long manicured nails and Botoxed foreheads. And both loved to gamble. Bobby Senior had taken three of the squares for himself, and Junior had two. They sat at the bar with their entourage, front and center to the big-screen TV, drinking whisky on the rocks and yelling at the screen.

"Pass, pass, *pass!*" Spittle flew from Senior's lips. The

quarterback got sacked, and half the crowd groaned while the other half cheered.

"Gimme another, sweetheart," Junior said, pushing his glass forward. His girlfriend eyed Shanna suspiciously, as if every female in Junior's vicinity was trying to steal him away.

"You saving the rest of the bottle for yourself?" Junior demanded. Shanna glanced at Dan, who gave the slightest of nods, and she filled the glass to the top.

"That's more like it." Junior slurped whisky. His girlfriend sneered, sipping white zinfandel.

"Don't get uppity with the lady," his father admonished from the stool beside him. "You ain't got a dime I didn't give you. And don't expect me to pay your bookie when you lose big tonight."

"I got a feeling, Pop," Junior said, jiggling the ice cubes in his glass. "Tonight's my night."

Bobby Senior's forehead wrinkled in disgust. "Like you had a feeling about that broad who turned out to be a cop? Got us both thrown in jail with that *feeling*, Numb Nuts. I'm telling you, if you're in over your head, that's on you. Don't come begging me to bail you out."

Junior glowered at his father but said nothing.

"Hey, Squid!" Abel yelled across the packed room. "Who you like for the win?"

Billy the Squid looked up, startled, as he always did when someone addressed him directly. "I guess New York," he muttered. Although his scratchy voice could barely be heard over the din, his answer was met with boos and catcalls.

"Figures," Charlie Mullins called. "The Squid just jinxed the Super Bowl!"

The crowd guffawed at the Squid's expense, but the rummy just shrugged his shoulders and went back to staring at the big screen, used to the abuse.

While everyone else was absorbed in the game, Shanna slid a bottle of Labatt's in front of him. "On the house," she said.

With a shaky hand, he gripped the bottle, giving her a grateful smile.

"How about that last drive?" Dan asked, turning the doorknob, letting the morning light pierce the gloom of the Strange Bird.

"I was *this* close"—Charlie pinched his fat fingers together— "to winning the final."

They filed into the room and surveyed the damage from the previous evening. The Squid snored softly at the bar.

Beer bottles, plastic cups, and used napkins were strewn over the bar and tables and floor.

"Slobs," Dan said. "My customers are a bunch of slobs."

"Yeah, well, they probably ain't feeling so hot today." Charlie checked his watch. "Hurry up, the bank opens in five minutes."

"Can you believe Bobby Senior won the final?" Dan made his way over to the coffee machine.

"Money goes where money is," Charlie replied. Despite the bulk of his belly, the outline of his .357 Magnum was visible on his hip.

"His son didn't look too happy. He was making furious phone calls after the game. I think he made some bad bets."

"He's been living off Bobby Senior's reputation for too long," Charlie observed.

"I'll get the lockbox out of the office. Senior won't want to wait for his money. With my luck, he'll show up early." Dan checked the time on his phone. "Damn, we better get a move on. I'll make coffee when we get back."

He disappeared into the office, came out a minute later with the steel lockbox under one arm. "I got the cleaners coming at three o'clock, so we can open at five. Let's get to the bank, Charlie."

There was a loud pounding at the front door.

"Who's there?" Dan lifted his head from a puddle of drool on the bar. The last thing he remembered was locking the payout money from the bank in the office and making a pot of coffee. "What time is it?"

Charlie rubbed his eyes and checked his watch. "Son of a bitch, it's noon. We must've fell asleep. We were more hung over than we thought."

Pulling himself together, Dan opened the door to an impatient Bobby Balzano Senior.

"You're hard of hearing when it's time to pay up, huh?" Though the temperature hovered around eighty, Senior had his jacket zipped up. A thick gold chain peeked out from his neckline.

"I got all the winners coming in staggered," Dan replied. "Nobody wants people knowing their business, especially if they owe certain individuals a debt or two."

"Like my good-for-nothing son," Senior snarled. "He lost big on the game, and I ain't seen his mooching ass all day."

Dan looked around. "I haven't seen my new barmaid, either, and she was supposed to be here at eleven. Maybe she's my ex-barmaid now." He fished his keys out of his pocket. "I'll be back in a minute."

He unlocked the office door and slipped inside.

"Not feeling so good?" Bobby asked Charlie, taking a stool.

"A little green around the gills," Charlie admitted. "You bought a lot of rounds, last night. Me and Dan passed out on the bar."

Senior nodded in commiseration. "Sorry about that. I just wanted to share my good fortune. A hundred and fifty thousand bucks is something to celebrate, even for me."

Dan's "back in a minute" stretched to two, then three, then five.

"Everything all right in there?" Charlie called.

"No," Dan said, coming out of the office with the lockbox in one hand and half a key dangling from a chain in the other. "Everything is *not* all right. The key wouldn't turn, and I twisted

121

it so hard it snapped off."

"Let's pry the sucker open," Senior said. He took the box from Dan and examined the jagged remains of the key jamming the lock. "I got a crowbar in my trunk."

Half an hour later, the three sweaty men stood around the intact steel box. Senior's crowbar had pried its sides up slightly, but it remained shut tight. Dan's hair had come loose from its ponytail and hung in stringy strands around his shiny face.

Frustrated, Dan brought the crowbar down onto the lid. Once, twice, three times, without making a dent in the steel.

"I think you killed it," Senior said, his own bald head glistening with a sheen of sweat as he took the tool from Dan's hand.

"This thing came from Home Depot, not Fort Knox," Charlie said, reaching under his golf shirt and pulling out his gun. "Let's go out back and introduce it to my little friend."

The Strange Bird was situated between a Cuban restaurant and a tattoo parlor, neither of which was open so early in the day. The three men tramped into the little patch of sand, dirt and rocks that made up the bar's fenced-in back yard and put the box smack in the center.

"Stand back," Charlie cautioned them, aiming his cannon directly at the lock, "and plug your ears."

The sound of the gun going off was deafening.

"What the *hell*?" screamed Dan.

Dollar-sized pieces of paper floated through the air, but they were cut-up newsprint, not money.

Some still sat in the box, wrapped to resemble stacks of hundred-dollar bills. It was no stretch to imagine that there were exactly three hundred thousand fake dollars there in front of them.

Dan fell to his knees and spilled out the rest of the box's contents, hoping the real money was in there somewhere. "Fucking Abel! He was in yesterday and saw where I keep the lockbox."

"Coulda been your new bartender," Charlie pointed out. "She didn't show up today." A piece of newspaper settled on his white Velcro sneaker, and he kicked it off.

"It could have been my son," said Senior. "This is right up that good-for-nothing's alley. But I don't care who stole it. *They* don't owe it to me." He pointed the crowbar at Dan's chest. "*You* do."

"Hold on." Dan put up his hands. "Charlie, help me out here."

Charlie stepped between the two men, the .357 still in his hand but down by his thigh. "Let's all take a deep breath. Bobby, you'll get your money. Dan's been running this pool for fifteen years and never stiffed nobody. He'll just need some time to figure this out."

"There's nothing to figure out. I want my money. *Now.*"

"I can't turn newspaper into cash, Bobby," Dan said. "You see what happened here, right? I was robbed."

"I'm going to find Carla Haskins, Jimmy Kinski, and Ricky Santana," Senior said. They were the other big winners, who would be showing up to collect their prizes any minute. "Let's see how they feel about this."

"You gotta give me some time!" Dan was pleading now. Jimmy Kinski was six-five and a former boxer.

"You got forty-eight hours," Senior said. "After that, your ass is grass and I'm the lawn mower."

"No need for threats," Charlie said.

"This ain't no threat," Senior said, waving the crowbar. "I want my money, and I'm going to get it, one way or another."

He didn't wait for a response, just stomped out of the yard, still carrying the crowbar.

In the distance, a siren howled.

"Sounds like somebody called in the gunshot," Senior growled over his shoulder. "Too bad you can't report the theft of illegal football pool funds."

Charlie let out the breath he was holding.

"What do we do now?" Dan wailed.

"We've got two days to figure it out," Charlie said. "If we can't find Bobby's money by then, we'll have to get the hell out of Dodge."

Two days later, they had packed their bags and were holed up at Dan's bungalow. They'd turned off their phones after the first threatening call and hadn't left the house or talked to anyone since. Dan had no idea if Shanna had ever shown up, no clue if Junior had resurfaced or what had become of Abel.

Despite twenty-nine years of police experience, Charlie couldn't piece together who'd taken the money. Hell, the lockbox hadn't even been full until they'd emptied out the safe-deposit box at the bank that morning. He'd watched Dan lock the box in the office. The only person with a key to the office was Dan. And the only person with a key to the lockbox was also Dan, who wore it around his neck. It was a real whodunit, all right.

Their plan now was to get in Dan's car, haul ass up Route 1, get off the Keys and past Miami and out of Florida altogether.

"Let's go," Charlie said. It was just past eight a.m., and he didn't trust Senior to give them the full forty-eight hours he'd promised.

Dan grabbed his duffel bag, and the doorbell rang.

"Get down," Charlie whispered. Pulling his gun, he crept toward the front window.

"Who is it?" Dan hissed.

"FedEx," Charlie said, letting the curtain drop.

"How do you know? Maybe it's a setup!" Dan was wedged under his dining-room table, holding his duffel bag against his chest like a shield.

"Unless Bobby Senior owns a FedEx truck, it's FedEx." Charlie cracked the front door open a sliver.

"Dan Faulkner?" the uniformed driver asked in a bored voice.

"That's me," Charlie told him.

The guy shoved an envelope into Charlie's hand. "Have a nice day," he said.

"What is it?" Dan asked, climbing out from beneath the table.

"It's a letter." Charlie turned it over in his hands. "From Mexico."

"Mexico?" Dan snatched the envelope. "I don't know anyone in Mexico."

Sliding a finger under the flap, he tore it open.

The two of them read the neat block printing together:

Dear Dan (and Charlie, if you're reading over his shoulder)—

If this letter seems a little all over the place, it's because I hired young Juan from the marina here in this little town on the Sea of Cortez to get it on paper for me.

I've been planning to steal the pool money for two years now, since that first time you called me Billy the Squid.

I'm sorry Bobby Senior lost out on his hundred and fifty grand, but, hey, he never missed a chance to have a laugh at my expense.

You made it pretty easy for me. The lockbox was the key to the whole thing. Remember last year, I asked if I could hold it after you and Charlie came back from the bank, just to get a feel for how much it would weigh? Did you know you can order the exact same lockbox on Amazon for less than a hundred bucks?

Anyway, on Hangover Monday I let you and Charlie pick up the money from the bank like always, and while you were gone, I spiked your sugar bowl with crushed-up sleeping pills. A lot of them. I was afraid I might have used too many, but you were both breathing when I took off with the box, so I hope you're okay.

Remember that heavy backpack I had? That was my lockbox, filled with stacks of cut-up paper. I substituted mine for yours.

Then, while you two beauties slept, I slipped a fake key onto your chain and tucked it back around your neck. I dumped the rest of the sugar in the sink and washed out the bowl and refilled it.

I wish I could have seen you guys trying to open that box with the dummy key. What'd you finally do? Run it over with a truck? Smash it with a rock?

Anyway, the fake box bought me enough time to catch the ferry to Tampa. From there, I hired a puddle jumper to fly me here—you'll understand if I don't tell you the name of the town—where I bought a bottle of tequila and a beautiful little cabin cruiser I'm gonna rename 'No Comprehendo.'

I guess you're in a world of trouble, Dan—you, too, Charlie, if you're reading this. If I was sober, I might even feel sorry for the both of you.

But as I sit here watching the sun set from the deck of my new floating home, I think I'll just make me and Juan another Margarita. I'll have him put the finishing touches on this letter, since my eyes aren't focusing too good. Tomorrow, I'll have him express it to you from town.

Oh, P.S. I left ten grand in an envelope taped to the Bird's front door for your new barmaid. I wrote her she should get out of Key West as fast as she could. I hope she took my advice.

One Particular Harbour
Released 1983

"Stars on the Water"
"I Used to Have Money One Time"
"Livin' It Up"
"California Promises"
"One Particular Harbour"
"Why You Wanna Hurt My Heart?"
"Honey Do"
"We Are the People Our Parents Warned Us About"
"Brown Eyed Girl"
"Distantly in Love"

All songs by Jimmy Buffett,
except "Stars on the Water" (by Rodney Crowell),
"I Used to Have Money One Time" and
"Honey Do" (both with Michael Utley),
"Livin' It Up" (with Josh Leo and J.D. Souther),
"California Promises" (by Steve Goodman),
"One Particular Harbour" (with Bobby Holcomb),
"Why You Wanna Hurt My Heart?" (by Arthur Neville),
and "Brown Eyed Girl" (by Van Morrison).

WE ARE THE PEOPLE OUR PARENTS WARNED US ABOUT

Elaine Viets

When I saw the letter from the CEO of Truman Auto Parts in my inbox, my heart pounded like a Chevy with a blown head gasket. What made it scary was it looked so official: heavy cream stationery, fancy logo.

Might as well get it over with, I thought. Hands trembling like a man on a three-day bender, I tore open the envelope.

"Dear Vincent Fowler," the letter began.

Turns out it was one of those good-news/bad-news deals. The good news was I wasn't being busted for boosting. The bad news was I was out of a job.

I'd worked for TAP for thirty years, and I admit I skimmed a bit out of the register from time to time. But, hell, they hadn't given me a raise in a decade. Armbruster J. Truman III made thirty-two million dollars a year for manning a desk, so I figured I was entitled to a *little* something extra.

The company would never miss it. My store was the top-selling parts place in Humbert, Iowa, a town of fifty thousand about ninety miles south of Des Moines. I gave Truman a fair day's work and—thanks to my initiative—went home with a fair day's pay. Weekends, I played guitar in a Jimmy Buffett cover band at

Ronnie's Roadhouse, picked up beer money and a little more. I met my wife Sue at Ronnie's. She was a server on the weekends, on top of her regular job at an insurance agency.

Armbruster J. the Third's letter informed me that TAP would be closing its Humbert location in two weeks, leaving twenty-five of us unemployed. As a consolation, he promised me three thousand dollars in severance pay. Big whoop.

It was hotter than the hinges of hell when I locked up at nine-thirty that night. At home, Sue met me with a cold beer. She's pushing forty and even prettier today than when we married ten years ago. She has big brown eyes, soft, curly brown hair, and a sexy constellation of freckles on her right shoulder. I've made a lot of stupid mistakes in my life, but marrying Sue was the smartest thing I've ever done.

She didn't take the news I was being canned the way I'd expected.

"This is a blessing in disguise," she said, perching on the arm of my recliner. "I've been dreading another Iowa winter. What would you think about moving to Florida?"

"Florida?"

"We don't have any reason to stay here, no kids or close relatives. I've always wanted to live in Fort Lauderdale."

"I like Florida," I said. "But it's hot there in the summer."

She kissed my sweating forehead. "It's been over a hundred degrees *here* for four days straight."

She had me there.

"The TV weatherman fried an egg on the sidewalk on tonight's news," she said. "It's going to stay this hot through September. Let's try living in Lauderdale for a month. If we can stand the heat in August, we can stand it any time. We'll use that three thousand dollars to relocate. What do you say?"

When I came home the next Monday, she said, "I found us a cute rental apartment on Coconut Isle, a man-made island off

Las Olas. It's right on a canal! We can walk to the ocean. I took it for a month."

On Tuesday, she said, "I was talking with Betty Bradford in Muscatine. She wants to move here to spend more time with her mother. She's always liked our house and might be interested in buying it."

On Wednesday, Sue said, "Betty will rent our house for the month of August. If we decide to stay in Florida, she'll buy it— *furnished*. We can buy all new furniture there."

On Thursday, she said, "Nick Flynn will handle the house sale, if we go ahead with it. And he'll only charge us half his regular fee."

On Friday, my last day of work, Sue picked me up at the shop. The car was packed and gassed up. We cashed my final paycheck and severance check and waved good-bye to the corn-fields of Iowa.

We enjoyed the three-day drive south, listened to Jimmy Buffett songs all the way. When we hit Fort Lauderdale, we found Coconut Isle, a well-manicured finger of land that stuck out into the Intracoastal Waterway. Number Nine, where we were staying, was a long one-story building painted bright white and trimmed in tropical turquoise. The green lawn was shaded by palm trees, and at the dock in the back bobbed a beautiful white thirty-foot Hatteras cabin cruiser. The boat's name was lettered on the stern in gold paint: Leaky Tiki. When I saw that, I thought I'd died and gone to heaven.

Sue and I got out of our car and just stood there, admiring our surroundings: the gleaming white boat, the blue water, the rustling palm trees. It was like walking into a tourist brochure.

A guy about my age came out of the boat's cabin with a smile on his face. "I'm Gardner Puckett," he said, and stuck out his hand for me to shake. "Are you our new tenants?"

We introduced ourselves, and Gardner invited us on board

for a Cajun martini. Sue's face positively glowed. This was the life she'd dreamed about. Yes, it was hot, but there was a cool breeze off the water. And a cool drink—several of them, in fact. When Gardner's wife Kaye came home, she joined us on deck, and the four of us toasted the setting sun.

We really hit it off with our landlords. About seven o'clock, Kaye said, "I've got some burgers in the fridge. How about if we throw them on the grill?"

Sue went inside to help, and Gardner and I stayed on the boat, drinking martinis. He fired up the grill. Gardner was a letter carrier, and Kaye worked for the Social Security Administration.

They were generous hosts, and we had a delicious dinner of burgers, potato salad, sliced tomatoes, and chocolate cake, all the while listening to Jimmy B. tunes: "Cheeseburger in Paradise," "Come Monday," and Gardner's personal favorite, "We Are the People Our Parents Warned Us About," after which he'd named their boat.

As the drinks kept coming, I got my guitar from the car, and soon we were all singing along. It was midnight by the time Sue and I were ready for bed, and we were too tipsy to unload. We tottered into our new apartment and didn't wake up until noon.

Kaye had thoughtfully stocked the kitchen with bread, butter, eggs, and coffee, and the late breakfast Sue prepared saved my hungover life.

After breakfast, I hauled our stuff out of the car, and Sue unpacked. While she settled us in, I went for a walk. The salt air was invigorating. Next door was Coconut Isle Park, a pretty pocket park with three benches and a huge ficus tree. The rest of the block was residential. The other buildings were similar to Gardner and Kaye's: white houses with one or more rental units. About halfway down, I saw a gaunt older woman in a blue flowered housedress raking her lawn. She wore a floppy straw hat, and her strong hands were knotted with veins.

"Good afternoon," I said.

She leaned on her rake and said, "Afternoon. And who might you be?"

"I'm Vinnie Fowler. My wife Sue and I are renting Number Nine from Gardner and Kaye Puckett."

The woman froze. Even her frizzy gray hair didn't move. "What do you think of them?" she asked. She sounded cautious.

"They're terrific," I said. "We spent the evening partying with them."

"Hmph," she said. "Where are you and your wife from?"

"Iowa."

"Figures," she said. "You seem nice enough. Maybe too nice for your own good. Let me give you a word of warning: you can party on their boat as much as you want, as long as it's at the dock, but don't ever go on a cruise with them. The last fella did that, he never came back. He was from Michigan."

"Why?" I asked.

"Why didn't he come back? Or why was he from Michigan? I can't answer that last question, but as to why he didn't come back, my guess is he crossed those two somehow and they tossed him overboard. The crabs got to his body, and there wasn't much left. Look it up. His name was Everding. Elmore Everding. It was in the papers."

Suddenly, despite the August sun, I felt cold.

"Uh, thank you," I said, backing away.

"You're welcome," she said. "He was a nice friendly guy like you before he became fish food."

I waved good-bye and noticed the woman had two rental units behind her house. I tried to tell myself she was a competitor of Kaye and Gardner's, but I didn't quite believe it.

Back at our place, Sue was so happy I thought she'd bust. I didn't say anything about the conversation I'd had on my walk, but a thought gnawed at me: how could Gardner and Kaye afford this big house and that fine boat on two government salaries? The taxes and upkeep alone ought to have wiped out their paychecks.

As the month rolled on, our money disappeared at an alarming rate. Sue found a part-time job as a waitress, and I went to work at a hardware store. We agreed that we weren't going back to Iowa.

One night after dinner, we found our ideal house: a two-bedroom Caribbean cottage with—I swear—a white picket fence. I'm about the last guy who ever thought he'd want a house with a picket fence, but Sue fell in love with the place, and I had to admit it was pretty. It was painted a soft yellow with white trim, set on a little canal, with a big mango tree in the yard.

"We can pick our own mangoes and have them for breakfast," Sue said.

The house was for sale at what in Fort Lauderdale was a bargain price, but a Fort Lauderdale bargain was not the same as an Iowa bargain. If Betty bought our house in Humbert, we'd clear enough for the down payment, but I had no idea how we could keep up with the mortgage when our new jobs paid so little.

"Maybe Gardner and Kaye have some ideas," Sue said. "You could ask him."

Asking people about their finances is pretty personal, so I held off until one night at a cookout, when Gardner was pretty well oiled. After we finished the best barbecued ribs I'd had in a long time, Gardner and I offered to help do the dishes, but the ladies said they had it under control and shooed us out of the kitchen. Personally, I think they wanted some girl talk.

So Gardner mixed another batch of martinis, and we sat on the deck of his boat. A light breeze kept the mosquitoes away.

"Gardner," I said, "I've got to hand it to you. You and Kaye manage to live like kings on a couple of civil-servants' salaries. How do you do it?"

Gardner's slightly bloodshot eyes shifted from the cabin cruiser to the house and rental unit, then to the whispering palm trees.

"Well, Vinnie, I guess I'm just one lucky S-O-B. Kaye inherited the house and the rental unit from her father when he died in 1997. The rental gives us a nice little cash boost. You know that."

Boy, did we ever. We were paying two thousand a month for a one-bedroom in the off-season. During the winter months, when the snowbirds came to town, the rent went up to three grand.

"As for the boat, we got that after Hurricane Wilma. It was damaged—we picked it up cheap—and I restored it. What you're looking at is the result of many nights and weekends of hard labor." He waved his martini glass at the nautical-themed pillows and upholstery and the shining mahogany deck.

That all made sense, I guess, but not quite. I had the odd feeling my new friend was holding something back.

Then again, so was I. I didn't mention Elmore Everding.

That night in bed with Sue, I told her what I'd learned.

"Hard to believe," Sue said.

"I agree."

"Gardner and Kaye live in one of the richest sections of Fort Lauderdale, and this property needs constant upkeep. Kaye said they're going to have the house painted next month. And I won't begin to guess what their taxes are. I guess they're better at managing money than we are."

I wasn't convinced. But Sue, who always has a plan for every-thing, said, "I think we should start saving our change. I get a lot of tips, and they add up."

"We're going to pay the mortgage in quarters?"

"You can laugh, but it was my tip money that paid for gas and meals on the trip down here."

Now I'd hurt her feelings. I felt like a rat. "You're right, honey," I said. I kissed her, and she kissed me back, and soon we forgot all about how Kaye and Gardner made their money.

Our idyllic month was nearly at an end. Sue was in love with Florida and wouldn't hear a word against it—she even claimed to like the humidity. "It's good for your skin," she said.

I continued to worry about our landlords, but I said nothing to my wife. We had dinner with Gardner and Kaye almost every night, and they were fun to be with—kind and witty and always entertaining.

We still hadn't figured out how we would buy our dream cottage, but Sue was optimistic. "Something will happen," she said. "I just feel it."

I felt something, too, but it was an ominous heaviness in the pit of my stomach.

One afternoon—the last of the month we'd paid for—I came back from the hardware store and found Sue pacing in the driveway. As I pulled in, I saw she was white-faced and shaking. She practically dragged me out of the car.

"Honey, what's wrong?"

"Look in the mailbox!" she said.

At the end of the drive was a plain black mailbox mounted on a black metal post.

"Betty promised to send me an offer on our house. I checked the mail, and you won't believe what's in there! Look!"

I pulled open the box, and stuffed inside was a one-gallon plastic freezer bag fat with what I believe the police call a "green leafy substance." In other words, pot. Nearly four pounds of it, by my estimate.

"*That's* how Kaye and Gardner can afford all this," Sue said. "They're drug dealers! What are we gonna do?"

I put my arms around her. "We're not going to do anything. We leave tomorrow morning. We'll stay at the Residence Inn until we find a more permanent place."

"But they're having a good-bye party for us tonight. I can't go. I can't look at them after this."

She started crying. I hugged her and patted her slightly sweaty back.

While I did, I formulated a plan. Sue had been right. Something would happen, she'd said, and it certainly *had*—and we could use it.

I whipped out my cell phone and took pictures of the mailbox and its contents. "Are you sure you put the bag back exactly the way it was?"

"Yes! No! I don't know."

I guess you're wondering why Sue was making such a big deal over a package of pot. Well, neither one of us is an angel, but we don't use illegal drugs. We don't judge people who like their weed, it's just not our thing. And we had never encountered a dealer before.

"You don't have to go to the party," I said. "I'll tell Gardner and Kaye you ate some bad fish for lunch and have an upset stomach. You go inside and close the curtains and get some rest. I'll handle this."

I checked online and found a website, FreeAdvice Legal, that said possession of marijuana is generally illegal in Florida. *Medical* marijuana seemed to be permitted for personal use, but you had to have a "debilitating medical condition," which included things like cancer, epilepsy, and multiple sclerosis. So far as I knew, Gardner and Kaye were healthy as horses, and the law defined personal use as twenty grams or less—not four pounds.

Another piece of free advice caught my eye: "You do not have to be caught in the act of selling marijuana to be charged with attempted distribution." Possession of twenty-five pounds of pot or less within a thousand feet of a park or school was a felony with a maximum of fifteen years in prison and a ten-thousand-dollar fine.

Next I searched for information on the late Elmore Everding. A headline said, "Suspected Drug Dealer Found Dead in Fort Lauderdale Canal." The article was short: "The badly decomposed body of Elmore Everding, 37, was found in a canal off Las Olas Boulevard today. Mr. Everding, a former resident of Addison, Michigan, lived on SW 13th Street in Fort Lauderdale. Police sources say he was a low-level drug dealer and may have been involved in a territorial dispute over drugs. Police say Mr. Everding was struck on the back of the head and fell or was thrown into the water. Results of the autopsy are pending."

Was Elmore trying to break into Kaye and Gardner's business—if they had a business? Or did they abruptly terminate a partnership with him? I'd find out tonight, I thought.

Meanwhile, I needed evidence. I made sure my cell phone was charged, grabbed a bottle of water, and walked to the pocket park next door. At five-thirty, the hot afternoon was starting to cool off. I sat on the bench beneath the ficus tree, where I had a clear view of the Pucketts' mailbox. I set my camera on video mode. Fifteen minutes later, a red BMW pulled up. A man in a business suit got out, opened the mailbox, took out the bag of pot, and left a thick manila envelope in its place.

I made sure I got several good shots of the car's license plate as it drove off. Two minutes later, Kaye came out of the house like a shot. She opened the mailbox and grabbed the envelope. It slipped out of her hands and fell to the concrete driveway, where it burst open. Money spilled out, a lot of it. Kaye scooped it up and hurried back inside.

I got the whole thing on video. Gardner might not care about himself, but he'd do whatever was necessary to protect Kaye.

I called our friend Nick in Iowa, asked if I could email him some notes and a video file, and made him promise not to open the message unless he hadn't heard from me within the next two days.

"Everything okay down there, buddy?"

"Fine," I said. "This is just a little insurance. We may never need it."

But I *did* need a weapon. Though we usually drank Cajun martinis at Kaye and Gardner's, tonight I'd switch to beer. If I knocked the neck off a bottle...well, I'd seen enough bar fights at Ronnie's Roadhouse, I knew the damage a broken beer bottle could do.

I went into our apartment to get my wallet.

"Where are you going, honey?" Sue asked.

"Thought I'd pick up some beer," I said.

"Take my quarters," she said. "I have four rolls on the dresser."

I bagged the rolls in a clean black sock and stuck it in my pocket.

At the supermarket, I bought a six-pack of Heineken. By the time I got to Kaye and Gardner's with a fake smile plastered on my face, it was five minutes to seven.

"Hey, hey," Kaye said. "Where's your better half?"

"She's not feeling well," I said. "She ate some bad fish for lunch."

"That's a shame," Kaye said.

"Hope she's better soon," Gardner said. "You switching to beer?"

"Just had a taste for it."

"It's warm," he said. "Let me put it in the cooler. Meanwhile, have a martini."

He handed me a frosty one in a plastic cup—Gardner didn't like glass on his boat—and I pretended to sip it.

Kaye stood up and said, "I have some things to finish in the kitchen. I'll let you boys talk."

As she sashayed toward the house, Gardner said, "How was your last day? Anything unusual happen?"

"Nope," I said. "Just another day in Paradise."

"What about your little kerfuffle at the mailbox?" he said, with a big Cheshire-cat grin.

"What—?"

"Don't bother to deny it," Gardner said. "I have cameras everywhere."

Of course he did. I looked around and saw the red lights, like demons' eyes, winking from the deck, the covered patio, the palm trees, and by the mailbox at the end of the drive. I cursed myself for getting soft, now that we'd moved to the tropics. I was used to working with cameras: they had them all over the parts store back in Humbert. I'd personally disabled the one by the register, and the cheapskates had never fixed it. Hah! That had cost them a pretty penny.

But now my carelessness was going to cost me my life.

"I saw the way your wife reacted to that bag of mulch in the mailbox," he said, laughing.

"That wasn't mulch," I said.

"It'll look like mulch in the photo you took with your cell phone."

"Maybe, but what about the green stuff that landed all over your driveway when Kaye dropped the envelope? I got that on camera, too—*and* your customer's plate."

Gardner looked surprised, but he recovered quickly. "Well, I've got your wife," he said. He fished a key out of his pocket, and I looked into his slitty mean eyes. "By now, Kaye's bolted the doors to your unit from the outside. We have the only two keys. So what do you say you and me go for a cruise and have a little talk?"

I remembered what the woman up the street had warned me: don't go out on Gardner's boat.

"I get seasick," I said. "I'm from Iowa. Biggest body of water I like is a bathtub. That's why I didn't sign up for the Naval Academy, like my parents wanted."

"If you ever want to see your wife again, you'll go for a ride," he said. He had a gun in his hand, and he handled it like he knew how to use it.

I tried to look brave. "Can I have a beer now?"

"No. Sit down and shut up." He jabbed me in the back with the gun, and I sat.

"Don't even think about leaving," he said, "or your wife will die."

He went into the cabin to start the engine, and I looked around frantically for a weapon. I could hit him with a deck chair. But he had a gun.

I slapped my pockets, checking for my car keys. I could poke him in the eye with a key—but he had a gun.

Wait a minute. Sue's quarters. I'd paid for the beer with a

credit card, so they were still in my pocket. Four rolls of quarters in a sock would make a powerful weapon.

I splashed the rest of my martini on the deck. The engine sputtered to life, and Gardner reappeared.

"Hey!" he said, slipping on the puddle of martini. I walloped him good and hard with the sock full of quarters, and he went down like a sack of feed. I took his gun away and killed the engine. Then I opened myself a beer and sat there with his gun, waiting for him to wake up.

"What happened?" he moaned at last. Then he saw the gun in my hand. "You son of a bitch!"

"That's no way to talk about your new partner," I said. "Now here's how this is going to work. I emailed the video I shot of Kaye to my lawyer in Iowa, and if he doesn't hear from me, he'll send it to the Fort Lauderdale police and the D-E-A. You're looking at fifteen years and a ten-thousand-dollar fine, Gardner, plus extra time since you've been dealing drugs within a thousand feet of a park. Oh, and using a mailbox as a drug drop, that's a federal crime. I'm surprised a mail carrier didn't know that."

He rubbed his head and tried to sit up. "What do you want?"

"I want fifty percent of your gross."

"Thirty," he said.

"You really want to bargain with Kaye's freedom? Fifty."

"Okay," he said.

"No tricks, now. Remember, if anything happens to me, my lawyer will send that incriminating video to the cops, along with a suggestion they check this boat for Elmore Everding's DNA. He had a head wound, so he must have done some bleeding. A little Luminol will light that blood right up, no matter how many times you washed the deck. Now give me that key, and I'll let my wife out."

I tossed his gun into the water, locked him in the cabin and set Sue free. She was already packed. We loaded our car and headed for the Residence Inn.

* * *

Sue and I kept our jobs. I got promoted to full-time at the hardware store, and she was soon working fifty hours a week at the restaurant. Our bosses loved what they called our "Midwest work ethic," which in South Florida meant we showed up on time. We sold our house in Humbert to Betty and used the proceeds as a down payment on our dream cottage.

Sue and I never barbecued with Gardner and Kaye again, and we both felt bad about that. But not too bad. The money was rolling in. Gardner had a good situation. He sold pot to the people who sold pot to the young professionals downtown, nice white folks who smoked a little weed in their homes.

I promised Gardner that, as soon as we paid off the mortgage on the cottage and had a hundred-thousand-dollar nest egg, I'd dissolve our partnership and destroy the video of his wife. He wants rid of me, so I figure we should reach that benchmark in a year or two. Meanwhile, I check in with Nick once a week, just for insurance.

Eventually, Florida will legalize marijuana, and then there'll be no need for people like Gardner and me.

But in the meantime, well, we *are* the people our parents warned us about.

Riddles in the Sand
Released 1984

"Who's the Blonde Stranger?"
"When the Wildlife Betrays Me"
"Ragtop Day"
"She's Going Out of My Mind"
"Bigger Than the Both of Us"
"Knees of My Heart"
"Come to the Moon"
"Love in Decline"
"Burn That Bridge"
"La Vie Dansante"

All songs by Jimmy Buffett,
except "She's Going Out of My Mind" (by Mac McAnally)
and "Bigger Than the Both of Us" (by Rhonda Coullet).
The first three and last five songs on the album were co-written
with Michael Utley and Will Jennings
(and, on "Who's The Blonde Stranger?," Josh Leo).

WHO'S THE BLONDE STRANGER?

Robert J. Randisi

Stackhouse stared up at the Hotel Galvez.

He had never been to Galveston before. In fact, he had only been to Dallas and Fort Worth in the past. As a rule, he hated Texas. He hadn't even liked the long-running television show *Dallas*. So when his friend Temple asked him to come to Galveston for a possible job, he had second thoughts. But in the end, he agreed, and Temple told him he'd have a room waiting for him in the Hotel Galvez.

He checked his watch, saw that he was due down in the bar to meet with Temple. They had worked many jobs together, but it had been some time since they'd seen each other. Years ago, they'd discovered that they didn't hate each other as much as they hated most people.

The bar was busy with what looked like a combination of spring-breakers and businessmen and women having lunch. Temple was sitting alone at a table off to the side with a drink in his hand. When he saw Stackhouse approaching, he smiled and stood up. Stackhouse noticed that Temple had put on weight since he'd last seen him, but not much.

"You want a drink," Temple asked, as they shook hands, "or are you still not drinkin' when you work?"

* * *

"I ain't workin' yet, am I?" Stackhouse asked. A waitress came over, and he ordered a Shiner Bock—the only thing he liked about Texas—while Temple had another Jack and water.

"This can't be Texas," Stackhouse said. "Looks like fuckin' Florida."

"I know," Temple said. "When we come down here from the ranch, it totally blows my mind."

"We?"

"Me and the wife."

"You got married?" Stackhouse asked, surprised. "I never thought I'd see that day."

"Yeah, I know," Temple said, leaning forward. "Me, neither. But, see, that's why I called you down here."

He fell silent and sat back as the waitress put their drinks on the table, then leaned forward again when she left.

"What's the problem with your little lady?" Stackhouse asked.

"She's missin'."

"They got PIs for that, Temple."

"I don't need a PI," Temple said. "I need a handyman. I need *you*. I'm willin' to pay your goin' rate."

"Are you okay, Temp?"

"I'm good," the man said. "I'm just worried about Lola. That's my wife."

"Lola," Stackhouse said.

"We met four years ago, honeymooned down here, and we come back every year. We got in two nights ago, and now she's gone. I called you yesterday, but I didn't think you'd get here so fast."

"I took a private helicopter from El Paso. You sounded—desperate."

"You dropped everythin' to come help me?"

"I had nothin' goin', and you did say you were gonna pay me. I'm thinkin' I can give you the 'friend and family' rate."

"You don't have any family," Temple pointed out.

"So you're the lucky friend who gets the discount." They drank to that and ordered another round.

"She said she was gonna have a drink with a friend in the bar," Temple said, "and then come to bed. I fell asleep. When I woke up yesterday mornin', she wasn't there."

"Why call me, Temp?" Stackhouse asked. "Why not the police or somebody from Dallas?"

"The cops would've laughed. One look at my sheet and they'd just figure I got what I deserved. We haven't seen each other in a few years, Stack, but you're still the only person I trust. Plus, you don't have a rap sheet. At least, you didn't the last time I saw you."

"Still don't," Stackhouse said.

"Anybody I would've brought down here from Dallas would," Temple said.

"I get it," Stackhouse said, "So put me in the picture."

Stackhouse took Temple's key card—one of those plastic things you just wave at the lock—and went up to his old friend's room. A "Do Not Disturb" sign was hanging on the doorknob.

He doubted Lola was missing. It was more likely she'd gone off with some sun-bleached beach boy for a little fling. In his experience, the seven-year-itch was a myth: husbands and wives had the itch all the time. It was just a question of whether or not they were strong enough not to scratch it. Stackhouse was betting Lola wasn't.

He searched the room, which didn't take long. It was a typical hotel setup, with a king bed, sofa, writing desk, chest of drawers, and flat-screen TV. The drawers were filled with frilly things and a collection of tacky bikinis, except for one crammed with Temple's stuff. Same thing with the closet: mostly a woman's jackets and dresses, some men's things shoved off to one side. Temple was obviously one of those men who deferred to his woman. Stackhouse was sure Lola also claimed ninety percent of the closet space in their house. That was why Stackhouse didn't think he could ever live with a woman. He liked his closets and drawers too much.

He went into the bathroom, found the counter covered with women's items for hair and skin care. In a corner was a man's comb, toothbrush, and deodorant.

There was nothing to tell him where Lola might have gone or with whom.

He left the room and found a housekeeping cart. Inside were two maids cleaning and chatting.

"Excuse me, ladies," he said from the doorway.

They turned and looked at him, surprised. He knew his size had that effect on people, especially women. He smiled to put them at ease.

"Would one of you be in charge of cleanin' room sixteen-oh-two?"

The older one raised her hand. "That would be me, sir, except they leave the Do Not Disturb out all the time."

"You haven't been in the room since they got here?"

"No, sir. But—"

"But?"

"I stopped by yesterday to see if they wanted towels, and I heard them screaming at each other, so I didn't even knock."

"Did you hear what they were sayin'?"

She looked at her friend.

"Tell him, Nancy," the other girl said. "He's probably a policeman."

"Did something happen?" Nancy asked.

"The lady in that room is missing," he said. "I'm trying to find her."

The two women exchanged another glance.

"Is there somethin' else?" Stackhouse asked.

"The first night they were here," Nancy said, "they had a fight in the bar."

"How do you know that?"

"We know Diane, the waitress who was working that night," Nancy said. "She told us."

"Did she tell you what they were fightin' about?"

"You should ask her," Nancy said, "and Paul, the bartender."

"Are they on duty now?"

Nancy checked her watch. "It's two o'clock. They come on at four."

Stackhouse used the time to get himself a room and unpack his small overnight bag. He stowed everything away in a dresser drawer, except his .45. There was a small safe in the room, and he put the gun there.

The bar wasn't large, had only half a dozen tables. The bartender was young, barely older than a spring-breaker. He looked as if he shaved only once every eleven days.

Stackhouse took a stool, his size drawing the bartender's eye. Moving about the small room was a brunette waitress he hoped was Diane.

"Get you a drink?" the bartender asked.

"Shiner Bock, on draft."

When the bartender set a frosty mug in front of him, Stackhouse asked, "Are you Paul?"

"That's right," the bartender said.

Stackhouse put his key card on the bar. "Room ten-oh-five."

"I'll start a tab."

Stackhouse took a swallow. "Is that Diane?"

"That's right," Paul said. "Do you memorize names?"

"Not exactly," Stackhouse said. "There's somethin' I need to talk to the two of you about."

"Are you some kind of cop?" Paul asked.

"No," Stackhouse said, "but I'm lookin' for a missin' guest."

"So a private eye, then?"

"Somethin' like that."

Diane came to the bar with an empty tray.

"This fella wants to talk to us about a missin' guest," Paul said.

The girl gave Stackhouse a pretty smile. "You're a big one, ain'tcha? I dig the bald head."

"Thanks. I understand you two witnessed a fight between two guests a couple of nights ago."

"Which one's missin'?"

"The wife."

Diane and Paul exchanged a glance.

"What was that?" Stackhouse asked.

"What was what?"

"That look," Stackhouse said. "It meant somethin'."

"We better tell him," Diane said. "The wife? She's seein' one of our locals. He calls himself Ranger. We don't know his real name. He's a blond surfer-dude type, lives in a shack down the beach."

"Is she with him now?" Stackhouse asked.

"I don't know," Diane said.

"Tell me how to get there," Stackhouse said, "and I'll go and check."

Diane walked him to the doors that led to the beach. "Just head that way and you'll come to it."

"Thanks," Stackhouse said.

"Before you go, there's somethin' else you should know. The husband, he's been foolin' around, too."

The shack looked pretty sturdy, had a solid front door and a shuttered window. Stackhouse tried the door, found it locked.

"Hello?" he called, banging on the door.

No answer.

"Lola, come on, I know you're in there! Temple sent me."

Still no answer.

He looked out at the water and saw no one swimming or surfing.

"I'm comin' in," he shouted.

The door was solid, but Stackhouse was six-and-a-half feet tall and weighed almost three hundred pounds. The NFL and the WWE had both wanted him, but neither football nor wrestling had appealed to him. Law enforcement had, but following someone else's rules didn't. So he'd become a handyman and hired out to whomever could pay him. He had worked for local police, federal and international agencies, a bad guy or two. A door on a beach shack wasn't much of a challenge.

He put his shoulder to it twice before it cracked open. He went in two steps and stopped just short of a puddle of blood.

A blond man and a woman who fit Lola's description were on the floor, clad in shiny black wetsuits.

There was no need to check their pulses. He could see they were dead. When he heard the sirens, he knew he had to get out of there.

He headed up the beach, away from the hotel, hoping the police wouldn't come from both directions.

He found a stairway and took it up to the road. He started walking toward the hotel and saw a crowd of police and paramedics outside the shack.

Stackhouse made it through the lobby to the bar without being seen by the cops. He grabbed Diane's arm and pulled her aside.

"What happened?" she asked.

"You tell me," he said.

"What do you mean?"

"Did you know they were dead?"

"They—they're *dead*?" Her eyes were so wide Stackhouse was fairly certain her surprise was genuine.

"Who told you to send me there?" he asked.

"Nobody. I—I thought I was helpin'."

"Tell me more about the husband and the woman he's seein'."

"Just some blonde," she said. "I don't know who she is, but they were in the bar together the day after we saw the fight."

"What were they doin'?"

"Well, they were sittin' together, but in this job, you get so's you can read body language."

"And?"

"And I figured they were, you know, doin' it."

"So you think they were *both* cheatin'?"

She hesitated.

"What, Diane?"

"Well, what I said about body language?"

"Yeah."

"The wife and Ranger, they didn't have it."

"So you don't think *they* were cheatin'?" Stackhouse asked.

"I don't know, maybe. But he gives surfin' lessons, so—"

Stackhouse thought back to the shack. There were surfboards all around, and both bodies were wearing wetsuits.

"Sonofabitch."

"I'm sorry, did I—"

"Not you," he said. "You've been real helpful."

"Mister, are the cops lookin' for you?"

"I believe they are," he said.

"But you didn't kill 'em, did you?"

"I did not—but I've got a pretty good idea who did."

Temple answered Stackhouse's knock in a bathrobe with the hotel's initials on it.

"You sonofabitch," Stackhouse said, shoving the man back, "you set me up."

"I did what?"

"You killed your wife and her blond lover and set me up to take the fall."

"I don't know what you're talkin' about," Temple said. "Wait, Lola's dead?"

"Don't play innocent with me, Temp," Stackhouse said. "You knew I'd find them in that beach shack, and you called the cops, figurin' I'd get caught."

"Why the hell would I do that?" Temple asked.

"Because you've got yourself a new side-piece," Stackhouse said, "and Texas is a community property state."

"You're crazy, Stack," Temple said. "Why would I do that to you? You're my friend."

"Which is why you knew I'd come runnin' to help you."

Temple stuck both hands in the robe's pockets.

"Temp, if you come out with a gun, I'll feed it to you," Stackhouse said. "And you know I can do it."

"Look, Stack—"

The bathroom door opened, and a beautiful young blonde— also in a hotel bathrobe—stepped out and pointed a gun at Stackhouse.

"Try feeding it to *me*, big boy," she challenged.

"Wow, Temp, this one's got fire," Stackhouse said. "I really think she'd use that thing. But then there's millions involved here, right?"

"Don't listen to him, sweetie," the girl said. "You know I love you for you."

"Come on, Temp," Stackhouse said. "When has a woman ever loved you for you? Did Lola? Does this one?"

"Shut up!" the woman snapped.

"Tell me, did you kill Lola and her surf instructor, or did she?"

"He was her lover!" Temp insisted.

"No, he wasn't her lover," Stackhouse said, "but this beauty was yours. You're the one who was cheatin', not poor Lola. She just wanted to learn to surf."

"Don't listen to him, baby," the woman said. "I'm gonna shoot 'im."

"Go ahead," Stackhouse said. "You ever try to move a

153

three-hundred-pound body?" He looked at Temple. "You remember that guy we hadda move in San Antone that time? Damn near broke our backs."

"He's right," Temple said. "You can't kill him here."

"So we'll take him somewhere else, then. We'll take turns gettin' dressed and holdin' the gun on him."

Stackhouse looked at the blond stranger and watched her mind working. Her hand was steady, but he knew Temp's wouldn't be. Whenever they'd worked together in the past, Stackhouse had done the dirty work, and Temp had helped with the clean-up. Until Temp had hit it big in the lottery, anyway. All that money had put some distance between them.

"I'm willing to bet you Lola was a gold digger, and so's this one," Stackhouse said. "I mean, come on, man, look in the mirror. Ain't neither one of us a hunk, ya know. You and me, we *pay* for girls like this."

"Temp," the girl said, her tone holding a warning.

"I know pinnin' this on me wasn't your idea," Stackhouse said.

"I guess it was, Stack," Temp said. "We needed a patsy. I couldn't think of anybody else to call, man. I'm sorry."

"Yeah," Stackhouse said, "so am I." He turned to the girl. "What's your name?"

"Debbie."

"Well, come on, then, Debbie," he said. "Do it. Shoot me."

"You said—"

"I know what I said. It'll be loud, and I'll be heavy. But you're gonna have to do it, or I'm gonna take that gun away from you."

Stackhouse took a step toward her.

"Shoot him!" Temple yelled. "Shoot him, Deb!"

She hesitated just long enough for Stackhouse to reach out and grab the gun from her hand. He backhanded her, sending her flying into the bathroom. Then he closed the door.

"Here's what you're gonna do," he said. "Call the cops, tell 'em you got the woman who killed your wife locked in your bathroom."

"In a bathrobe?"

"Tell them you've been bangin' her, and when you refused to leave your wife, she killed her and her surfing instructor."

"But," Temple asked, "don't you wanna know if she really did it?"

"I don't care," Stackhouse said. "All I care about is that they don't think *I* did it. Did you give 'em my name when you called 'em?"

"No."

"My description?"

"Yeah."

"Okay, then," Stackhouse said, "I've gotta get out of here." He waved the gun at Temple. "You get this done, Temp. If you don't, you're dead."

Temple hung his head.

"This new bitch only wants your money, you know that."

"I guess."

"How much did you win again?"

"A million a year for twenty years."

"And that was five years ago?"

"Right."

"I'm guessin' you ain't got the whole five million squirreled away."

"No."

"How much?"

"Maybe a couple," Temple said.

"You went through three million dollars?"

Temple shrugged. "I bought houses, boats, you know…things."

"Blondes? Jewelry?"

"That, too."

"I don't get it," Stackhouse said. "Why kill Lola in the first place? Wasn't she hot enough for you?"

"She was," Temple said, "but I made the mistake of marrying

her. When you marry 'em, women change."

"So this one you weren't gonna marry?"

"No."

"Just kill your wife for."

"Well…"

"Look," Stackhouse said, "in order to keep me from killin' *you*, you're gonna have to give the cops Debbie. And when this is all over, you can go out and buy yourself another blonde. Got it?"

"Yeah, I got it," Temple said. "I'm really sorry, Stack. She said—"

"Forget what she said. Just call the cops—and don't fuck with me!"

"Right, right."

"I'm gonna see if I can get out of this hotel without gettin' arrested," Stackhouse said. "Oh, one more thing."

"Yeah?"

"You're gonna pay me a hundred thousand dollars for my trouble—and don't you ever call me again!"

Last Mango in Paris
Released 1985

"Everybody's on the Run"
"Frank and Lola"
"The Perfect Partner"
"Please Bypass This Heart"
"Gypsies in the Palace"
"Desperation Samba (Halloween in Tijuana)"
"If the Phone Doesn't Ring, It's Me"
"Last Mango in Paris"
"Jolly Mon Sing"
"Beyond the End"

All songs co-written by Jimmy Buffett,
except "The Perfect Partner" (by Marshall Chapman).
Jimmy's collaborators on the other songs were: "Everybody's on the Run"
and "Last Mango in Paris" (Chapman, Will Jennings, and Michael Utley),
"Frank and Lola" (Steve Goodman),
"Please Bypass This Heart," "If the Phone Doesn't Ring, It's Me,"
and "Jolly Mon Sing" (Jennings and Utley),
"Gypsies in the Palace" (Glenn Frey and Jennings),
"Desperation Samba (Halloween in Tijuana)"
(Jennings and Timothy B. Schmit),
and "Beyond the End" (Chapman and Jennings).

EVERYBODY'S ON THE RUN

Laura Oles

A cloud of dust trails behind me as I make my way down the dirt road. My rearview mirror offers little in the way of compelling scenery. It's the same long stretch I've traveled over the last thirty miles, familiar and slightly hypnotic. Gypsy, my Australian Shepherd, rests his head on the bottom of the open passenger-side window, the wind blowing his patterned fur back. It's the middle of February now, so the southwestern Texas desert has been more forgiving during the day than she is in the summer months. The temperature is in the fifties, and I keep my window down to let cool air fill the cab. My mind drifts for a moment, away from current concerns, but not for long.

My brother Jack is in trouble.

Again.

Jack is a decent human being with a knack for making bad decisions. He's one of those people who has to learn things the hard way. Some folks see red coils and know the stove is hot. Jack needs to put a finger on it to make sure.

Even though he was born first, Jack is the baby of the family, so it feels like I'm his "big" sister. Somehow, the universe jumbled up our birth order, and it's been a tough go ever since. I don't fault the higher powers entirely; our family's foundation is built on generations of bad decisions.

159

I roll up my window, and warmth returns. Flecks of dust drift in the air, settle on the dash. I haven't passed another vehicle in miles, but that isn't unusual. Our cabin is near Terlingua, a remote Texas town that has in recent years become a tourist attraction. Its mining history and ghost-town status draw curious vacationers just long enough to snap a few photos for their Instagram stories.

My grandfather used to say people who come here are either running *from* something or searching *for* something.

The Donnamore clan checked both boxes.

The cabin is our family's beacon, the place my brother and I regroup during times of crisis. My grandfather built it, back when men built their own houses, and the structure is solid.

I walk up the shallow steps, reminding myself we need to fix the railing one day. Gypsy runs off into the brush, in search of adventure. Inside, I drop my duffle and check the fridge.

I turn on the TV and can't believe my luck: one of my favorite movies is on. I'm twenty minutes in when I hear a car pull up outside. The engine cuts, a door slams, and there's Jack.

"How's it going, little brother?"

His dark hair has grown long, and his right eye offers hints of a punch still healing. "Guy was a leftie, eh?"

He smiles at the jab, hugs me and grunts. "Ribs are going to take longer to heal. *The Maltese Falcon*, eh? Good one."

I nod. "Keep your eye on that O'Shaughnessy dame. She's crafty." I pat the couch. "Sit."

Jack retrieves a beer left over from our last visit and sits. His body is stiff, and his right foot taps the floor. He's never been one to relax, his energy level always a few notches above everyone else's.

"Cheers," I say.

He gives me a clink and takes a long draw. "I'm sorry to drag you out here."

I pat his knee. "No problem. My home life is unraveling at a record pace, anyway."

"Pete still drinking?"

I nod. "Getting worse. Time to get out. I can't sleep at night."

"Let's go sit on the porch," Jack says. "I need some fresh air."

We move outside and take in the vastness of the land around us. I feel exposed yet safe, both at the same time.

I watch Gypsy duck in and out of the desert brush, searching for things to chase. Jack sighs the way you do when you're getting ready to deliver bad news. For the first time in years, I see real fear in his eyes. His shoulders slouch, and I can tell he's trying to find the right words. The longer he takes, the more scared I get.

"How bad is it?" I ask, not sure I want to know.

His eyes stay focused on the bottle in his hands. "I have a week to come up with a hundred K, or things are going to get really ugly." He looks up at me. "Maybe for both of us."

My beer sours in my mouth. "Both of us?"

"I told you about that job I got driving shipments?" He takes a long drink from his bottle. "Well, I got jacked. They knew what I was carrying, and I'm on the hook for the full value of the load."

I lean forward and rest my elbows on my knees. I take a few deep breaths to calm the panic building in my chest. "How is this your fault?"

Jack offers the hint of a smile, but the tension in his jaw tells another story. "Lex, you know my line of work. It's my job to deliver, and I got sloppy."

Jack has always been on the run from something. His jobs, which keep him moving from city to city, are about more than the work. He *wants* to live this way, regardless of the risk. I think the risk is what fuels him, even more than the promise of fast cash.

"And how do I figure in?"

He bows his head. "They know about you, Lex. Our families are how they keep us in line."

We sit quietly for a few minutes, my mind racing with ideas, plans, ways to fix this. That's my role in our relationship: I'm the one who fixes things, cleans up Jack's messes.

But this?

"We need to go see Vonne," I say.

He nods and sighs. "I know, but I don't trust her."

"Neither do I, but we don't have any choice."

I lean back beside him, our shoulders touching, eyes ahead on the desert that surrounds us. Gypsy darts across the gravel, chasing a rabbit.

I know how the rabbit feels.

Vonne Mason glanced at her watch as she sorted through a stack of papers. Never a fan of computers, she preferred to handle her bookkeeping the old-fashioned way. The RV park, situated on the outskirts of Presidio, attracted those souls looking for a life off the grid. Names optional, cash only, a month's rent up front.

She stepped outside to inspect the sky's intentions. It often promised rain but rarely delivered. She heard a vehicle in the distance, held up a hand and squinted at the road. A black Suburban came into view. New model, more square than rounded, tinted windows. An unusual sighting in an area known more for El Caminos and banger trucks than slick SUVs.

Vonne reached inside her shirt pocket for a cigarette. She wasn't expecting company, and she wondered if she ought to fetch Mabel, her trusty Glock 19. Too late now.

The SUV slued to a stop in front of her trailer. Its engine quieted, its driver remained behind the wheel. The rear passenger door opened, snakeskin boots touched gravel, and a cowboy hat emerged. Vonne wondered if Boss Hogg had come calling.

"How're you doing, Vonne?" the stranger asked, his eyes smiling in an unfriendly way. She didn't like him already.

"I'd be doing better if I knew how you know my name," Vonne replied, taking a drag off her cigarette.

He waved the comment aside.

"What can I do for you, Mr.—?"

He patted the front of his starched button-down shirt, the

buttons holding in a well-fed midsection that spilled over his ornate silver-tooled belt buckle. "I'm Jimmy Flair—and, yes, that's my real name."

"And why are you on my property, Mr. Jimmy Flair?"

Flair came up the steps, and they stood eye to eye, Flair all soft and fair, Vonne with her weathered skin and hands that had known decades of hard work.

"Here's the thing, Ms. Mason," Flair said. "I have a business proposition for you."

"What makes you think I'd be interested in doing business with you?" Vonne stubbed out her cigarette with the heel of her boot.

"I'd like to buy this land from you for a project I have in the works, and I will pay you a fair price for it."

Vonne shifted her weight. "I'll pass, Jimmy Flair. I've got money of my own, and I sure as hell don't need yours."

Flair handed Vonne a business card, which she took with reluctance. "I think you should reconsider. If you don't, some of my colleagues are going to pay you a call, and they won't be nice like me."

"Get off my land," Vonne cautioned. She turned her back on him and returned to her office and watched the SUV drive away.

Jimmy Flair and his "colleagues" were going to have to be dealt with, somehow.

We're back in my truck, Jack at the wheel, and I can tell Gypsy is nervous. When Jack is working, he follows every traffic law, risks nothing—but driving for personal reasons brings out the Andretti in him. I can feel the truck's frame rattle in the desert wind.

"Slow it down a bit, okay?" I say. "You're scaring my dog."

He grimaces like a teenager annoyed by a parent's cautious words, but he eases his foot off the gas. I've always been the string on his kite, even times when I longed to float away myself.

I glance at the dashboard clock. Twenty minutes more on 170 before the turnoff.

"Whatever happened with that girl? What was her name, Emily?"

Jack shrugs, keeps his eyes on the road. "She didn't like my line of work."

"Ran like the wind and never looked back?"

He smirks at me and reaches over to give me a poke in my side. We both know he's not built for relationships. Neither of us is.

Vonne's RV park is ninety minutes from Terlingua, a run to the store by Texas standards. She's the only family—and I use the term loosely—we have still in the Lone Star State.

Still, the devil you know...

Jack pulls up on the gravel pad and cuts the engine. As soon as I open the door, Gypsy makes a run for it. Jack and I get out and look up at the trailer. The screen door fills with a woman's outline.

I go first and greet Vonne through the metal mesh that separates us. A cigarette dangles from her hand. She takes a drag and blows smoke at us.

"Been a while," I say. I step inside, Jack right behind me.

"Really? I didn't notice you were gone."

"Good to see you, Auntie V," Jack says, looking around the modest structure. He raps on the service counter, which I imagine is the source of very little service. "How's business?"

"Good. Steady. Lots of long-timers." Vonne taps ash into a black plastic ashtray, the kind you'd see in a dive bar.

"We've been driving for a bit," Jack says. "How about a beer? And don't tell me your fridge isn't stocked. I know better."

Vonne nods. Sometimes I think she has a soft spot for Jack, but then my childhood memories remind me that's not true.

She comes back from the kitchenette with three cans of Natty Light. We pop tops and drink, just another day at the office.

"Get to it," Vonne says.

Jack and I exchange glances. I speak first. "We know you're still sitting on Grandad's take from that...thing he pulled...and we need our share."

Vonne raises a hand. "That money doesn't belong to you two. Your Uncle Wayne did the heavy lifting, Lord rest his soul, and that money is ours. *Mine.*"

Jack steps in. "I've got some serious heat on me right now, V, the kind that makes a Terlingua summer feel like a Paris winter, and time is running out for me and Lex."

"I see you've dragged your sister into one of your messes, eh?" She seems amused by our plight, and that pisses me off. I resist the urge to lunge at her throat and just *take* the damn money, though I know she's too clever to keep it here.

"How much you need?"

"A hundred K."

Vonne whistles. "You really stepped in it this time." She crosses her arms. "I won't just *give* you my money for nothing, but I have a job needs doing, and I'll pay you to do it."

"What kind of job?" Jack asks. "Must be dangerous for that kind of money."

"Big money, big job." She sips her beer. "I've got a guy who wants my property, but I'm not interested in selling. He's threatening me with his goons."

Jack and I exchange glances. This is a big ask.

"You want us to make him go away?"

Vonne shrugs. "That would be nice."

The next day, we stop at a convenience store to pick up some snacks and sodas and two prepaid phones. In this area, burners are as easy to find as beef jerky. I pull a phone from its box and toss the trash in the back seat. Gypsy gives me the side eye: he doesn't like anything in his space. I dial the number on the business card Vonne gave me, and, after four rings, someone picks up.

"Hi, is this Mr. Flair?" I put the phone on speaker, so Jack can hear. I bump my pitch up an octave, and it annoys me to hear it. Still, shiny lures work, and I'm trying to land a big fish. Jack smiles at my ridiculous voice.

"Who am I speaking to?" the man says after a pause.

"This is Kate Moore. I heard you're interested in Vonne's property, and I might be able to help you."

"What makes you think I need help, Kate?" He sounds like someone's wimpy uncle at a barbeque.

I hesitate, as if I'm nervous about sharing this information. "She doesn't want to sell, but I know some things might convince her to change her mind."

"Interesting," he says. "Why don't you come by my office? I'll text you the address."

I tell him I'd prefer meeting in the evening, since I have to work all day, and he agrees. I hang up and smile. "That was easy."

"Easy part's over," my brother replies. "Now it gets interesting."

The address Flair sends me is sixty miles away. Jack drives, and neither Gypsy nor I is thrilled about it. We arrive, and I'm surprised to find Flair's office is in a dingy strip mall with vacant storefronts on either side. There's no business name on the door, just the number 401 in peeling white vinyl on frosted glass. It's just past nine, and the outdoor lighting leaves much to be desired. There's only one other vehicle in the lot, a white SUV.

"You ready?" Jack looks at me. "There's no going back after this."

"What choice do we have?" I ask. "It's him or us."

Jack nods, checks his piece, tucks it in the waistband of his jeans. I'm not armed. This is Jack's burden, and he insists he's going to carry it.

We get to the front door, and I pull the metal handle. Inside, we find a man in a starched shirt, big belt buckle, dress pants, boots, balding head. His smile comes and goes quickly when he sees I'm not alone.

"Mr. Flair?" I extend my hand. He steps forward and gives me a limp shake. "I'm Kate, and this is my brother Will."

"Kate doesn't have a car," Jack explains, "so she asked me to drive her. I hope that's okay."

Flair is clearly unhappy with my chaperone, but he waves us back to his office. "C'mon. I'm just catching up on some paperwork."

The office is cluttered with tchotchkes on the back bookshelf, and most of the floor space is consumed by a big wooden desk almost hidden beneath stacks of papers. Jack points to a photo on the wall.

"You catch that? Damn, that's a big fish."

Flair smiles. "Great week in Cancun. The Island Reserve Riviera is first class."

He waits for us to sit.

"All right," he says. "What's on your mind?"

Jack pulls his gun from his belt and points it at Flair, who raises his hands.

"Did Vonne send you?"

"She's not going to roll over just because you threaten her."

Flair looks at me.

I shrug. "It's not personal," I say.

"Is this about money? Because whatever she's offering, I can do better." His voice reveals a hint of a shake. "How much?"

"She's giving us a hundred," Jack says, almost too quickly.

"I'll double it," Flair says. "But she has got to go. I have a big project in the works, and she's the last thing standing in the way." He reaches for his desk drawer, and Jack takes a step closer.

"Take 'er easy," Flair says. He removes a brick of cash from the drawer and offers it to me. "A down payment," he says. "This is ten thousand dollars right here."

I take the cash and slip it into my bag.

Jack slowly lowers his weapon. "I never liked Vonne much, anyway," he says.

* * *

The next morning, I call Vonne.

"All taken care of," I tell her. I instruct her to have our money ready, because time is the enemy and Jack needs to get square with his people before they come after him. She needs time to get the cash, she says. "Come by around ten this evening. I'll keep the light on for you."

Jack and I get the cabin sorted and locked down. I realize I might never see it again.

My brother seems to read my mind and gives me a hug. "I'm sorry I dragged you into this."

I hug him back. He's family. I have no choice.

"Hey, maybe we can go to England, see the Royal Family like you always wanted. You can dance in front of Buckingham Palace."

I smile at the idea. I don't want to return to my old life, and, once Jack is in the clear, there's nothing keeping me in the States. I will miss him, and I will worry about him.

We lock up, toss our bags in my truck. Gypsy jumps in, and we're once again on the road. My stomach is a touch queasy, and I can see Jack is amped up, too, the way he grips the wheel.

We arrive at Vonne's trailer. True to her word—which she has rarely ever been—the front-porch light is on.

"You sure about this?" says Jack.

"What options do we have?"

He shakes his head. "None."

The trailer's door is locked.

Jack knocks, the sound of his knuckles echoing loudly in the open desert. He gives me a glance, and I nod. He puts his body into the door and busts it open.

I flip the switch on the wall, and the room floods with fluorescent light. We take a quick inventory. No papers on the counter. All surfaces are bare.

Vonne is gone.

She has left a yellow Post-it on the fridge:
I don't like you much, either.

"How the hell did she find out?" Jack demands, crumpling the paper and tossing it on the floor.

He rubs his eyes and sighs.

"What are we going to do about your people?" I ask. "All we have is Flair's 10-K."

"We need to get you settled someplace safe," Jack says.

I shake my head. "No, we're in this together."

He stares hard. "You sure?"

I nod. "You'll just mess things up again on your own."

We pull the broken door shut behind us. This time, I claim the driver's seat. Gypsy looks at me from the back and returns to his slumber. I start the engine and put the truck in reverse.

"I hear Baton Rouge is nice," Jack says.

I pull out of the trailer park, onto the open road.

Louisiana awaits.

Hot Water
Released 1988

"Homemade Music"
"Baby's Gone Shopping"
"Bring Back the Magic"
"My Barracuda"
"L'Aire de la Louisiane"
"Prince of Tides"
"Pre-You"
"King of Somewhere Hot"
"Great Heart"
"Smart Woman (In a Real Short Skirt)"
"That's What Living is to Me"

All songs by Jimmy Buffett,
except "Homemade Music" (with Michael Utley and Russell Kunkel),
"Bring Back the Magic" (with Will Jennings),
"My Barracuda" (with Michael Utley, Russell Kunkel, and Steve Cropper),
"L'Aire de la Louisiane" (by Jesse Winchester),
"Prince of Tides" (with Michael Utley),
"Pre-You" (with Ralph MacDonald and William Salter),
"King of Somewhere Hot" (with Ralph MacDonald,
William Salter, and Robert Greenidge),
"Great Heart" (by Johnny Clegg),
and "Smart Woman (In a Real Short Skirt)" (with Marshall Chapman).

SMART WOMAN (IN A REAL SHORT SKIRT)

Isabella Maldonado

Donovan Snell sat on a long wooden crate packed with submachine guns. His second-in-command, Lenny Drover, had nearly finished inventorying the weapons. This would be Snell's last shipment. Two days from now, he would turn the business over to Lenny and sail off on his brand-new yacht to spend the rest of his days enjoying clear Caribbean waters, ice-cold margaritas, and sexy *señoritas*.

Tilly Prue, his accountant, bustled into the stifling warehouse. She had all the curves of an overcooked soup chicken and probably just as much gristle. Spotting him, she headed his way.

He heaved a sigh and spoke under his breath to Lenny. "Why can't they invent a shaker that can mix two women into one?" He shifted his gaze to his latest girlfriend, Lupe, who perched on the edge of a nearby crate, filing her nails. "Put these two together, you got a perfect blend."

Lenny grunted. "Tilly's not much to look at, but she keeps the books straight and her mouth shut."

Lupe stood and stretched, revealing a delectable expanse of tan stomach.

"Lupe, however, is a different matter." Lenny watched her

approach. "Who cares if she can string a sentence together or not?"

Guadalupe Gomez was a fantasy, a bronze beauty with curves in all the right places, long luscious legs, and a really short skirt to show them off.

"*Hola, papi*," she said, her accent flavoring the words with a spice smooth as the rum from her island home. "You almost done packing that stuff?"

He stifled an eye roll. "*That stuff*, honey, is what makes your shopping trips possible." He shook his head. "No, I'm not done, and I won't be till tomorrow night."

She slid him a sexy pout. "So you can play tomorrow, then?"

"Sure, honey, sure." Once he had her on his yacht, they could play all she wanted.

A deep male voice interrupted their banter. "I'll play with you now if you want, sweet thing."

Snell rounded on his most annoying employee. "Shut up, P.B." If he didn't learn his place, the man was going to find himself on the wrong end of a Glock. He stood and got in P.B.'s face. "Keep your mind on your work and your paws off my woman."

P.B. raised his hands in mock surrender. "Kidding."

Snell gave him a venomous stare. "Use your muscles to load crates, not to flex for the ladies."

P.B. was short for Pretty Boy. The moniker fit the blond, tanned beach bum Lenny had brought into the business a couple of months earlier. He had dimples for brains, but women adored him.

"Excuse me, Mr. Snell," Tilly said. "I've uploaded the files to your database. Standard encryption and security protocols." She adjusted her thick glasses. "There is, however, a slight problem."

He turned to her. "I pay you so there won't be any problems, slight or otherwise."

"I understand, sir, but one of your suppliers says you shorted him ten thousand dollars."

He jammed meaty fists onto his hips. "Who?"

"Steve Patton," she said. "I wired the full amount to his offshore account last week." Her words tumbled out in a nervous rush. "The numbers match, and our books are balanced. The problem's not on our end."

He slid a palm over his balding pate. "So either Patton's lying, or someone intercepted that transfer before it arrived."

Tilly crossed her arms over her slender chest. "I'm looking into it, sir."

"Make it fast. I want to know if Patton's trying to gouge me."

She tilted her head. "I'm on it. Just wanted to let you know, in case Patton decides to pay us a visit."

Snell didn't trouble to hide his anger. "That would be very stupid on his part."

Lenny snorted. "Seriously, who would come after an arms dealer?" He motioned around the warehouse. "We got enough guns and ammo here to supply a small army."

Snell would make sure no one interfered with his final transaction. As soon as the last of the payments hit his account, he'd be gone. He still hadn't decided whether to take Lupe with him. She was smoking hot, but could he tolerate a ditzy broad for months on end in close quarters aboard a boat? He needed a woman with a brain like Tilly and a body like Lupe. Until he found her, he'd be stuck in bimbo limbo.

Jake Foster, an undercover detective in the Miami-Dade PD, tapped the surveillance photograph with the back of his pen. "Snell's planning to move the merchandise tomorrow night."

Foster's lieutenant, Hal Brock, gave him a hard stare. "You're sure you heard right?"

"They talk freely around me," Jake said, nodding. "They think I'm a muscle-headed idiot, call me Pretty Boy."

He had managed to get everyone to shorten the stupid nickname to P.B., but it had served its purpose. No one in Snell's crew took him seriously. Nor did anyone on the police department, for that matter. Pigeon-holed in the role of boy-toy because of his looks, he'd suffered one humiliating assignment after another. After this operation, he was done.

"That's two days sooner than we thought," Lieutenant Brock said. "We need time to coordinate with the Feds. Make sure they aren't working their own case against Snell."

Jake had seen no sign of any federal investigation or undercover agents. And he'd kept a damn sharp watch out for both. "We'll let some of the guns walk," he said, circumventing the familiar argument. "The Feds can track them. The buyers are all overseas, anyway, so it's not our jurisdiction—but this prick Snell is. We've finally got him, and I don't want him slipping away."

Sergeant Brooks nodded his agreement. "I've been in touch with the ATF and the other partners in our Fusion Center. They're preoccupied with a big operation somewhere else and told us to go ahead."

Jake faced the lieutenant and drove his point home. "If we wait, Snell will be on his yacht, guzzling cocktails, scarfing shrimp, and banging that spicy *señorita* of his by sundown tomorrow."

Lieutenant Brock appeared to mull it over. "You think we could work that angle?"

Jake couldn't hide his irritation. "What do you mean?"

"Bring Snell's girlfriend in." Lieutenant Brock shrugged. "Assuming she's not involved in any of his criminal activity, maybe she could help us."

Jake rolled his eyes. "Boss, you have no idea. Let me explain. Lupe is a total smoke show, but she's…well…uncomplicated."

Sergeant Sturgis sighed. "You're saying she's dumb."

"I wouldn't trust her to assist with intelligence gathering," Jake said. "Or with walking and chewing gum at the same time."

"Speaking of women," Brock said, stifling a grimace, "you had any luck with Snell's accountant?"

"Tilly Prue?" Jake snorted as he recalled the time he'd wasted on her over the past two weeks. "I tried flirting with her, flattering her, buying her dinner." He shook his head. "Nothing doing. Maybe she likes chicks."

"Or maybe some women don't care for pretty boys," Sturgis said. "Maybe she's attracted to brainy guys."

"Yeah, right." Jake grinned. "You think she could resist all this?" He swept a hand up and down his body.

They laughed.

Lieutenant Brock grew serious. "When exactly is the shipment supposed to go out?"

"Tomorrow at twenty-one-hundred hours," Jake said, then added, "I don't like nighttime operations. Let's put an ops plan together tonight and execute the raid at dawn."

"You want me to reach out to the FBI or ATF again to let them know?" Sergeant Sturgis asked.

Brock held up a hand. "After we make the arrest. I don't want them bigfooting us or telling us to stand down. They can pick the carcass clean when we're done."

Sturgis nodded. "Meanwhile, Pretty Boy, you keep working on Snell's accountant. She's obviously smart, and she knows all about his business. Cozy up to her, and we can turn her before anyone lawyers up."

"I'll take one for the team, boss," Jake said. "But you owe me."

Snell stroked Lupe's silky black hair with his sweaty palms. He loved touching her. His office in the corner of the warehouse offered a modicum of privacy, but not enough to shove everything off his desk and get busy with Lupe. She knew how to flirt and tease, tantalizing him with whispered promises she had yet to fulfill.

His latest obsession, he'd allowed her to string him along for weeks, relishing the game. He knew he would tire of her as soon as he possessed her, like a new car or yacht. For that reason alone, he'd extended the torment of anticipation. The chase excited him, and they both knew it. His eyes roved over her like a starving man gazing at a buffet. He licked his lips. She was the tasty treat he would finally devour tomorrow aboard his yacht.

Snell's pulse ratcheted up at the thought. Lupe would probably give him a heart attack, but what a way to go. He held out a shopping bag.

"You're going to look hot in this."

Her dark chocolate eyes widened. "*Ay, papi*, this is nice." She pulled out a tiny white bikini, gasped, and giggled. "I like."

Not for the first time, Snell wondered how a designer could charge a fortune for three miniscule triangles of fabric held together by the barest of threads.

Tilly's nasal voice jarred him back to the present moment. "Excuse me, Mr. Snell."

He stifled a groan. "What is it?"

"I need to speak with you."

Snell moved to one of the overstuffed chairs in front of his desk, plopped down, and pulled Lupe onto his lap. "I'm listening."

Tilly let out a disapproving sniff. "I finished checking the discrepancy in the payment to Steve Patton."

"And?" Snell drew out the word, not troubling to hide his impatience.

She threw an annoyed glance at Lupe. "This is for your ears only, sir."

Lupe pouted.

Snell narrowed his eyes at Tilly, who had never before displayed a flair for the dramatic. "Is this some sort of play for a pay raise? Because I don't have time for—"

"It's a stay-out-of-jail play," she snapped.

Snell blinked. Tilly had never before spoken to him like that. He stood up, dumping Lupe onto the cement floor. Ignoring her stream of Spanish expletives, he barked, "Leave us."

When Lupe had flounced out of his office, he rounded on his accountant. "What the hell are you talking about?"

She flushed. "When I was checking the transfer to Patton's

account, something about the routing system caught my eye. On a hunch, I followed the cyber breadcrumbs."

He clenched his fists. "Speak English."

"I bumped up against a firewall protecting information about the account receiving the funds," she explained patiently. "I recognized it. It's a trap, diverts anyone attempting to do research into a virtual cul-de-sac."

Snell scrunched his eyes closed. "And you've seen this before?"

"Once." She swallowed hard. "Right before federal agents charged a former associate of mine with money laundering and a host of other felonies."

He gaped at his accountant in dawning horror. "You're saying Patton is working for the Feds, and we wired those funds to an FBI account?"

"FBI, ATF, CIA, IRS." Tilly fluttered her bony hands. "Who knows?"

Sweat prickling his scalp, Snell recalled his last conversation with his supplier. "I told Patton we needed the weapons yesterday because the buyers were picking up the shipment in two days." His mouth went dry. "The Feds can't risk the buyers escaping with the weapons."

Now it was Tilly's turn to look confused. "Which means what?"

"Which means they're going to raid this warehouse *tomorrow*."

Her palm touched her throat. "What do we do?"

Snell cursed. "We clear this place out tonight." He stalked over to his desk, yanked open a drawer, and rummaged until he found a roll of antacids. "Who else knows about this?"

"Just you."

He let out a relieved breath. He couldn't let anyone find out he'd been tricked. Such a gross oversight would make him look incompetent. He jabbed a warning finger at Tilly. "Not a word to anyone else, understand?"

She bobbed her head like a flustered hen.

Snell popped two Rolaids into his mouth and chewed furiously. An idea began to take shape, and a grin spread across his face.

Tired from a long night working in the warehouse with his men, Snell waited and wondered. Would the Feds storm the warehouse at dawn in a sea of tactical black, swarm inside wearing raid jackets and waving search warrants? Or hunker behind their vehicles in the parking lot, shouting orders through a megaphone? He sat in his swivel chair in the center of the empty warehouse, facing the main entrance, prepared to greet his visitors.

His perimeter surveillance cameras had gone dark fifteen minutes ago. He figured the Feds had disabled the feed somehow, which was as good as an announcement of their presence. He'd never been raided and looked forward to seeing how it would go. He remembered movies and TV shows he'd seen. But unlike the bad guys on the screen, *he* had a plan.

The only warning was a barely perceptible grunt outside the warehouse door. An instant later, the door banged inward. Snell shot to his feet as three cylindrical canisters rolled in, clanking on the bare cement floor, spewing acrid plumes of smoke. Before he could react, the devices detonated with an ear-splitting crash and a light bright enough to burn his retinas. The flash and the noise reverberating off the metal walls rendered him momentarily deaf and blind.

He flung himself to the floor and instinctively tucked into a ball, hands mashed against his ears. Squinting through the haze, he could make out a stream of SWAT officers pouring in through the narrow doorway, shouting commands he couldn't understand over the ringing in his ears.

Snell blinked up at a mountain of a man in tactical gear towering over him, assault rifle trained at his chest. He'd been expecting the cops, but not this.

Cold gray eyes glared down at him. "Donovan Snell?"

He mustered a bit of defiance. "Who wants to know?"

The black-clad behemoth yanked him to his feet as a slender man with a gold shield clipped to his belt emerged from a cloud of smoke.

"Lieutenant Brock, Miami-Dade P-D. Donovan Snell, you're under arrest. I have search warrants for these premises and your home."

"Miami-Dade?" Snell repeated. *City* cops? Where were the Feds?

Brock leaned in, crowding him. "Where are the weapons, Snell?"

Snell grinned. "Search all you want. I'm an honest business-man."

"You're going down, Snell, unless you start talking." Brock's gaze raked the empty warehouse. "Where is everyone?"

"On vacation. I gave them the week off."

Tilly should have deleted his computer files and scrubbed the entire system by now. She would take her cut and go her own way before the cops showed up at her house. Everyone else would be waiting offshore on the yacht with the shipment of weapons. Including Lupe. Sweet, sexy Lupe in her white string bikini.

"That's funny," Brock said, "because the other half of our team just picked up Tilly leaving your home office. She had a one-way ticket to Brazil in her purse."

A wave of dread washed over him.

"My sergeant finished interviewing her a few minutes ago. He tells me she kept a bit of insurance for herself, a flash drive with everything we need to know. She's talking to an Assistant District Attorney right now." Brock smirked. "I think she'll cut a deal."

Snell closed his eyes and groaned.

Six hours later, P.B. smiled at Lupe, who handed him a margarita.

In her white bikini top and a very short skirt, she smelled of coconut-scented lotion and salt air. Gulls cawed overhead as the sun beat down on the yacht's upper deck. He raised the glass to his lips and took a sip. He couldn't let himself drink too much until after the transaction. Then he would get good and wasted.

P.B. had spent most of the night hauling weapon-filled crates onto Snell's yacht, aptly named *Hot Water*. After stashing the last pallet below deck, he'd joined Lenny at the rail to watch the shore recede as they headed out to meet the buyer at sea.

When Lenny ambled up to the bridge to check in with the captain, P.B. wasted no time hitting on Lupe. Once she learned her current protector would be doing a long stretch behind bars, she might decide to look elsewhere.

Perhaps in his direction.

It hadn't taken much to convince Lieutenant Brock to let him remain undercover after Tilly and her lawyer had cut a deal with the ADA. In exchange for a lighter sentence recommendation, she explained how she'd suspected Patton of working for the Feds and reported it to Snell. Neither of them ever suspected the pretty boy, and they still didn't know the truth.

No one did.

With P.B.'s cover still intact, his bosses had allowed him to board the yacht to meet the buyers. He wore a transponder concealed in a bulky wristwatch. One tap would send out a signal so the Miami-Dade PD's Aviation Unit, Special Response Team, and Marine Patrol could converge on their location to make the bust.

P.B. set down his drink and unbuckled his watch strap.

"Why you do this?" Lupe asked.

"Getting rid of excess baggage." He flung the timepiece over the gleaming chrome railing and watched it sink beneath the surface of the water.

Lupe tilted her head. "I do not understand."

"I'm taking over the operation, honey." He cleared his throat and addressed the crew and his fellow passengers. "Gentlemen, I have an announcement."

Lenny and the captain emerged from the bridge. The others all looked up.

"Snell won't be joining us," P.B. said loudly. "Neither will Tilly. They're both in police custody." He waited for the murmur of surprise to die down. "The good news is, we still have time to make this deal and get away clean. The bad news is, we won't be welcome back in the U.S. afterward."

Lenny lifted the hem of his Hawaiian shirt to display the grip of a semiautomatic pistol tucked under the brightly colored parrots printed on the front. "I don't think so, Pretty Boy."

P.B. had anticipated the move. At his nod, the pair of goons standing behind Lenny moved in tandem to seize him. In less than two seconds, they had disarmed their former boss's second-in-command.

Lenny struggled in their grasp. "What the hell do you think you're doing?"

P.B. answered for them. "They work for me now. Anyone who wants a cut of the deal can join us. Anyone who doesn't"—he gestured toward the rail—"gets to play water polo with the sharks."

P.B. had recruited the hired muscle first, sensing their loyalty could be purchased. It hadn't taken long to settle on a price. The only wild cards were the newly hired yacht crew.

No one knew P.B. was a cop, although he suspected word would get out soon enough once his superiors realized he'd gone rogue. For now, he wanted to be seen as the modern-day pirate he had become.

The skipper gave him a sardonic smile. "Nothing like a little mutiny on the high seas." He touched the bill of his cap in mock salute. "Your orders, sir?"

"Bring the ship about," P.B. said, relieved he didn't have to hold the man at gunpoint. "Head due east at full throttle. We should be at the new meeting point in less than twenty minutes."

The captain gave a curt nod and returned to the bridge.

Lupe sashayed over to P.B. and slid her hand into his. "So,

you are boss now?"

He smiled down at her, bracing himself as the yacht swung around. "That's right, baby. No more Snell. No more Lenny." He bent to brush a kiss against her lush red lips. "I'm your *papi* now."

Concern widened her soft brown eyes. "But what will you do with Lenny?"

"Ah, Lenny," P.B. mused. "I've always thought of him as a real *chum*."

Before he could explain the pun, the captain called down from the bridge. "Radar shows three vessels closing on us at high speed." He grimaced. "I'm not about to engage in a firefight, and we can't outrun them. We'd best prepare to surrender and be boarded."

P.B.'s mind spun, calculating variables. It had to be his department. How had they caught up to him so quickly?

An idea occurred to him. He would play off his mutiny as a misunderstanding, claim he'd thought he was supposed to meet the buyers and complete the transaction before the bust.

As quickly as it came, the thin ray of hope flickered. No way Brock would buy it. The PD had all the evidence they needed *without* a risky transaction involving international arms dealers.

He needed someone to corroborate his story. Someone with nothing to gain and everything to lose. Someone too airheaded to know she'd be implicating herself in the process.

He gave Lupe's hand a squeeze. "Listen, honey," he whispered. "The cops will be here soon. You need to tell them you came to me for help and I took over from Lenny because you asked me to."

"Why would I do that?"

"Because Lenny attacked you."

"No." She stood there, gorgeous as hell, blinking in the sun. "He didn't."

Damn. If brains were dynamite, she couldn't even blow her nose.

He spoke slowly, carefully enunciating each word. "That's not the point, sweetie pie. The point is that *you*"—he jabbed a finger at her—"need to back *me* up, or we will *all* go to jail. *Comprende?*"

She lifted a sardonic brow. "Oh, I understand perfectly," she said, without a trace of an accent. "But I don't think *you* do."

P.B.'s mouth went dry.

Her grip shifted on the hand that had been entwined with his, twisting it behind his back. "You're under arrest, Detective."

The crew surged into motion, disarming Snell's dumbstruck thugs and holding them at gunpoint with practiced efficiency.

"Let me introduce you to my team," Lupe said. "The captain is Special Agent Freeburn from the FBI. The First mate is Agent Kurlander from ATF. The others are from the ATF, FBI, and Homeland." They circulated around the deck, taking Snell's men into custody.

With P.B. securely cuffed, Lupe grasped his shoulders and turned him to face her. "And I am Supervisory Special Agent Erica Sanchez, FBI. This is my operation."

"No," P.B. said. "Not possible."

"Running a separate investigation while the police have someone undercover on the inside is challenging," she said. "But—as you can see—it's *quite* possible."

"You were doing a sting this whole time?" he said, going on the offensive. "We were supposed to work together. Was that just a load of bullshit you Feds shoveled to the locals?"

She got up in his face. "We're fine with partnering, as long as the cops we're working with aren't crooked."

He schooled his features into what he hoped passed for contrition. "Look, Lupe—I mean, Agent Sanchez—maybe we can work something out. You need my testimony against Snell, Lenny, and the rest of his guys, right?"

"Actually, thanks to Special Agent O'Hara, we don't."

"Special—?"

"You know her as Tilly Prue." Lupe smiled with the air of

someone taking great pleasure in twisting the knife. "She's a forensic accountant assigned to my task force. She's been tracking Snell's funds for the past six months." She gave him a wink. "She even spotted that little offshore account of yours I imagine your department knows nothing about."

His knees buckled. He'd been squirreling money away for months while he came up with the plan to con Snell, preparing a retirement that would be a damn sight better than any pension he would earn from twenty-five years of service.

Lupe studied him. "Let's see, you've gone through denial, anger, and bargaining. Can you skip the fourth stage and go straight to acceptance?"

He understood the reference. The five stages of grief. Very fitting, considering his fate. He lowered his head. "Could you at least explain how you pulled it off?"

Lupe regarded him a long moment. "A few of our recent operations in Miami were compromised. We traced the leak back to your department, but we couldn't identify the individual responsible. We decided to smoke him out."

His stomach clenched. He'd been making a little money on the side by providing tips to some of the local drug lords. Not all the time, not consistently, not traceably. Or so he'd thought.

"So you told us to go after Snell without you and put two undercover agents inside without telling us?"

"Until we figured out who the mole was, we couldn't trust anyone." Lupe shrugged. "Yesterday, I ordered Tilly—Agent O'Hara—to advise Snell that one of his suppliers might be an informant for the FBI. I figured Snell would expedite the sale, forcing whoever was working against us to make his move aboard the yacht, where we had everything under our control."

P.B. felt his jaw go slack. "Tilly set me up."

Lupe nodded. "And I took you down."

The roar of high-powered boats converging on their position split the air. When they pulled alongside *Hot Water* and cut their motors, P.B. gave his captor due credit. "You thought of everything, didn't you?"

"I'm a smart woman," she said, her cheeks dimpling in a smile, "in a real short skirt."

That she was—and those, Jake "P.B." Foster knew, were the most dangerous kind.

Off to See the Lizard
Released 1989

"Carnival World"
"Take Another Road"
"That's My Story and I'm Stickin' to It"
"Why the Things We Do"
"Gravity Storm"
"Off to See the Lizard"
"Boomerang Love"
"Strange Bird"
"I Wish Lunch Could Last Forever"
"The Pascagoula Run"
"Mermaid in the Night"
"Changing Channels"

"Boomerang Love" is by Jimmy Buffett,
and "Mermaid in the Night" is by Roger Guth and Jay Oliver.
All other songs are by Buffett and Oliver,
except "Take Another Road" and
"Why the Things We Do" (both with Guth and Oliver),
and "Changing Channels" (with Mac McAnally).

THE PASCAGOULA RUN

Jeffery Hess

Highway 90 stretched out like the black tongue of the devil himself, and we raced that red Jaguar straight into his mouth at a hundred miles an hour. Ragtop down. The moon and stars lit our path. I felt weightless. Memories of what we'd just done wrestled with thoughts of the things we might do next. My ears rang and my head swam, but I shut down the fear elbowing around my brain.

I was three months shy of my sixteenth birthday. Uncle Billy had promised he'd let me drive in the morning if we found an empty parking lot somewhere to prove I could handle the clutch.

Billy was my father's black-sheep younger brother and unlike my father in every respect. He had a horseshoe mustache that hung lower on the right side and the bloodshot eyes of a man you wouldn't trust around your daughters. He'd been a gunner's mate in the Navy during the war, while my father built the ships guys like Billy would sail around the world.

A few minutes into the ride, Billy steadied the wheel at the bottom with his knee and flipped open his Zippo to light a smoke. I didn't know right off if it was tobacco or pot, but I couldn't help feeling a little disappointed when his exhale hit me in the face. I reached for his pack in the console, keeping an eye on him for disapproval. Instead, he tossed me the lighter.

191

"It'll calm your nerves," he said over the rush of top-down air.

It was sticky hot even for late September, that stagnant time before the Gulf temperatures ease off and the heat no longer amplifies the moisture in the air.

I cupped flame to my cigarette the way Billy had done. Smoke exploded in my lungs and made me cough. After a second, smaller inhale, I sat back and exhaled. My heart beat a little easier in my chest.

Billy checked the rearview mirror. I checked the sideview, not knowing what I was looking for.

When we walked into the Stateline Bar an hour earlier, Billy pointed to the folding Case knife I wore in a holster on my belt. "Rednecking it these days?"

My hand covered the holster in a loving way. "I never leave home without my most prized possession."

"*That* thing?"

"Don't you remember? You gave me this knife."

Billy laughed. "That sounds like me. Cool."

"You really don't remember?"

"I don't remember a lot of things, Jimmy boy. Now let's go wet our beaks."

Into my second beer, I couldn't help worrying about going to hell. I knew what we were doing was wrong, but when an adult gives you the green light you don't look twice. I figured I couldn't get into trouble, since I was technically his responsibility. Still, the knowledge never left my mind that this was the kind of sinning that would send me to confession to light a candle and beg forgiveness.

I never understood the word "sultry" until that night in that bar.

I'd danced with girls my age plenty of times, but I'd never been touched the way one of the women in the Stateline rubbed my thigh. I was tall and broad for my age, but if she'd known I was only a kid, she might never would've groped me or bought me beers.

Another one, a redhead with a mole on her chin, felt me up. Not once or twice or casually, but fully, repeatedly, intentionally, and aggressively. I loved every minute of it. Her breath smelled like clove cigarettes and the whisky sours she drank one after the other.

"Your uncle is fine and all," she said, "but I'd like to teach you a thing or two. Give you a night you'll never forget." With that, she glued her lips to mine and tongue kissed me. Me and Annie Dennings had fooled around some, but *this* woman played a full game of pinball in my mouth. When we came up for air, I happened to look in Billy's direction and saw him having the same luck. I had three beers in me at that point and thought life couldn't get any better.

That's when the shining light around Billy grew dark in the shadow of two hulking dudes, most likely shipyard workers, with disapproval all over their faces. Once those fellas showed up, the girls backed off me and Billy.

"You boys better get," a brunette named Sharon said. She was the only one who hadn't rubbed up and down the front of my jeans.

Billy reached for her hand and kissed it, regal like.

That set the two yardbirds squawking.

Billy juked around a high-top table, grabbed my arm, and shoved me toward the door. He pushed me out into the humid night air between Mississippi, Alabama, and the Gulf of Mexico, kept shoving me until we were up to speed, sprinting toward the Jag, him snapping his fingers and saying, "C'mon, c'mon, c'mon."

As we hauled ass away from that mess, my skin quivered. It felt as if half the liquid in my body was boiling and the other half was freezing. I buckled my seatbelt low across my hips and tugged out the slack.

* * *

193

I always knew big fun was being had by guys like Uncle Billy, and I wanted to be like him.

If I'm honest with myself, I'd go so far as to say I'd wanted to *be* Billy ever since I was five years old. So much so, I dressed up as him six Halloweens in a row. Whenever anyone asked who I was supposed to be, I replied, "I'm Uncle Billy. A fast-talking, topside-walking sailor of the seven seas. If you can keep up and you've a bit of luck, we'll have a time that'll make you weak in the knees."

I thought that sounded like something Billy would say.

Many of the older housewives on our street knew me as an altar boy and Scout and didn't approve. One year, Mrs. Flaherty practically threw a roll of SweeTarts at me and slammed the door after I told her who I was supposed to be.

But a few of the younger mothers got a kick out of it. A woman on Green Street touched her throat as she laughed and asked me to say it again. She gave me a Hershey bar and a dollar bill and said, "You're going to be very popular someday. I guarantee you that, darlin'."

The Jag's tires sounded out a smooth and steady hum as we headed for Pascagoula, the city of my birth. Billy had a contact there who would help him sell the Jag.

"Why would you want to get rid of a car like this?" I asked.

"Not legally mine."

Air rushed over the windshield and flooded the seats with a swirl of wind, but even at that speed, we could hear each other just fine.

"You stole it?"

"Borrowed it."

"But you're planning to sell it?"

"Money's money."

I had not suspected Billy had stolen that red convertible, but once I found out, it kind of made things even more exciting.

"You going to buy another one with the money?"

"Haven't thought that far ahead. Was never a Boy Scout like you."

"Who'd you say you borrowed this car from?"

"Didn't say and won't." He crushed out his cigarette. "Nobody you need to know about. He owed me, so—"

"For what?"

"Nothing. Just a favor."

"That's some favor if he owed you this much."

"Damn straight, Jimmy boy," he said, checking the rearview mirror again.

"Damn straight," I said.

"We got one stop to make. I think you're going to like it."

There had been no end-goal stated when he'd picked me up, but the understanding was I'd be out all night, long enough to see the morning sun.

"Where to?" I asked.

"Well, I know this good old gal out in Moss Point." He looked me up and down. "You ready for the next level?"

I didn't know what the next level was, but beer coursed through every system in my body and I wanted more of everything.

"She owns a trailer court. Runs it as a brothel."

"Hell, yeah," I said, slapping the dashboard. "Step on it!"

Billy let out a howl aimed at the stars.

Headlights shined over our shoulders and out our windshield.

"A sedan, not a truck," Billy said, "but that don't mean nothing. Still could be yardbirds hefting bats and tire irons." He smiled around his cigarette and giggled and slapped his knee. After a quick wink, he turned to watch the road. "Other than that, the night's going pretty well," he said.

We laughed for a solid mile. "Them old boys were madder than hell." We roared again.

When Billy raked his fingers through his hair, I did the same. The more of his mannerisms I could memorize, the quicker I would become him. I nodded at damn near every word he spoke. "That's so cool," I said, far too many times.

The rest of the world seemed to go away. I got lightheaded, and goose bumps crept up my arms. *Be cool,* I told myself, looking out at the passing trees. With Billy at the wheel, there was nothing to worry about.

Billy killed the engine and coasted into a Gulf station.

"What are you doing?" I asked.

"We'll have to stop for gas sooner or later. And I'd rather know now."

"Know what?"

"We'll see."

The place seemed deserted, except for a lone desk lamp shining inside the storefront.

I followed Billy around the pumps to the trunk, which he popped open, revealing a carton of smokes and a TWA bag.

"What's in there?" I asked

He grabbed a fresh pack from the carton, snapped his fingers and pointed. "That right there is the engine that drives this crazy train."

"I thought the car did that."

"The car is just a conveyance." He slammed the trunk shut. "Never mind. Fill 'er up."

I started pumping gas. Billy leaned against the fender, arms crossed.

A sedan pulled up to the pump opposite ours. Its windows were tinted, so I couldn't see inside.

I covered the knife on my hip with the palm of my hand.

The driver and passenger opened their doors simultaneously and their boots hit the ground, but they were smaller than I'd expected. The driver had a shock of platinum hair, thick as polar-bear fur, cut into a flattop. The passenger had the same haircut, but brown, like mine.

Their faces were distinctly female and would have been attractive if not for the hateful expressions. They wore full makeup and suits like the ones in magazine ads of British businessmen drinking expensive gin.

I wasn't exactly sure that they were female. To this day, I wonder if all that beer sloshing in my gut had altered my perception of events.

Billy ambled over, slow and cocky. "He sent you two, huh?"

"Apparently so."

"Good to see you again."

"Cut the crap, Billy."

"Okay, hot stuff." Billy snapped his fingers and pointed at them. "Consider it cut."

"Who's your little accomplice?" the woman with the polar-bear hair asked.

"Leave him out of it, Bert. He's just a kid."

"A half-drunk kid who looks like he just got laid."

"Still just a kid," Billy said. "My nephew. Don't make him pay for my mistakes."

"Mr. Al will be happy to hear you admit you made a mistake."

"Well, it's a mistake now that you broads have caught up with me."

"You expect Mr. Al to blow off a vintage car like that?"

"I just wanted a few more days. For Jimmy."

"Best time of my life," I said.

"Is that right?" Bert asked. "You dumb enough to believe this scumbag could pile up enough cash doing his shit work at sea to pay for a car like that? And, let me guess, he's been flashing around a lot of cash, too, right?"

"He bought some drinks, but—"

"Yeah, that's Billy boy for you. Everybody's best friend."

"Stupid of you to involve a kid," the other woman said.

"Well, Sid, I didn't know you two would find me so quick."

"Like I said, stupid."

"Fair enough," Billy said. "But how 'bout for his sake we do things the easy way this one time?"

Everything in me wanted to think the easy way was going to happen, but that seemed too good to be true.

"Hey, kid," Bert said. "You stash any cash your uncle gave you lately?"

"Cash?" I asked, stalling, hiding my surprise at the depth of Billy's mess. "I don't know nothing about any cash. Scout's honor."

"I don't believe him," Sid said.

"Me, neither," Bert said, throwing a jab I couldn't dodge. Her fist connected with my mouth, which filled with blood. The taste of iron overpowered the beer that lingered on my gums and tongue. I didn't see stars, but I was no longer steady on my feet. I covered my face with my hands and said, "Shit."

Billy made a move for Bert, but Sid whacked Billy in the back of the head with the barrel of her revolver.

Just that fast, it was like the sweet taste of fresh cream curdled to buttermilk gone rancid.

Platinum-haired Bert moved more like a mechanical invention than a sentient being. Brown-haired Sid was angular and stiff as a bookcase.

Bert grabbed me in a headlock before I could duck away. At that time, I topped out at a buck thirty-five dripping wet, and it was no exaggeration that she had me by at least thirty pounds. I couldn't break free.

These chicks were tall. Big-boned. Sturdy, some might say.

In the chokehold, my airway restricted and motor function diminished by half, I scoured Billy's face for traces of fear but found none. If anything, a raised right cheek formed the dimple he called his lucky charm. I was as scared as I have ever been in my life, but Billy kept his half-assed smile and held his hands high. "Ladies, we can work this out."

Sid pointed her revolver at Billy's torso. He shuffled side to side and said, "C'mon, Sid. It doesn't need to go down like this."

I tugged at Bert's arm in a sort of panic until I realized my hands were free. I reached for my knife, pulled it out of the case on my hip, and flicked the blade open with my thumb. Maybe it was the beer buzz making me brave. Or maybe I was just being stupid.

I could've stabbed the big broad in the thigh. She would've let go, I bet, but her scream might've made the other one shoot Billy.

I'd practiced throwing that knife at a circle I'd drawn with a felt-tip marker on a live oak, but this was different. Trees can't fight back. These two could kill us if I missed.

My heart racing faster than it did on the Tilt-A-Whirl at the state fair, I threw the knife. The blade pierced the back of Sid's gun hand, and she dropped the revolver with the hellish cry of a feral wolf.

Billy lunged for the gun on the ground and grabbed it as Bert yanked me into position as a human shield.

"Drop it," she yelled at Billy.

"Now why would I do that?" he asked, aiming the gun.

"I'll choke out your boy."

"Then I'd have no reason not to shoot you. So go on and let him go."

Bert released me and ran to Sid, who was on one knee, the blade still piecing her palm.

Billy walked over, stepped on her wrist and tugged out my knife. "I'm seriously impressed, Jimmy boy," he said, holding both knife and gun.

Maybe that was why he'd given me that knife in the first place. Not for that specific act in that specific moment, but in case of *something* unexpected.

It would take more than confession and candles to keep me out of hell now.

"You said this would be easy," Sid wailed, staring at her hand. "And now I'm going to die."

"You're not going to die," Billy said.

"If we don't get this car back before Tuesday," Bert said,

"Mr. Al will pull the funding for her kid's daycare, and I'll have to go back to pole dancing."

"The car's in great shape." Billy snapped his fingers and pointed at the Jag. "Not a scratch on her and almost a full tank. And most of everything is in the trunk. You take the Jag, the cash, and the coke, and go get her hand looked at."

"Good Lord!" I yelled. "*That's* what's in the trunk?"

"Not now, Jimmy," Billy said.

"What about you?" Bert demanded.

Billy didn't hesitate. "Me and the kid go the other way in that piece of shit sedan you're driving."

"You'll still be in a stolen car."

"When Mr. Al gets his Jag back, the other car won't matter. Besides, Sid can't drive with that hole in her hand."

I pulled off my T-shirt and wrapped it around Sid's hand. "Keep it elevated," I said.

We got in the sedan they had been driving and took off.

"I didn't want to hurt anyone," I said, shirtless and sweaty, "but I had to do something."

Billy propped an elbow out his open window. "You kicked ass back there, Jimmy. Saved the day with that ninja knife throw. You not only stepped into the spotlight, you *nailed* it, no pun intended."

I was trying to keep a lid on the chaos of emotions raging between my brain and gut.

"Be proud," he said. "Chips were down, you stepped up big."

He looked me dead in the eye. He seemed to have aged a decade since our night began. He looked like my father around the eyes, maybe more so than ever.

I wanted to take the knife and throw it at him.

He said, "Always knew you had it in you, boy."

That was his way of thanking me, though I saw it as a sign of weakness—needing a kid to save his ass. And what the hell was he thinking, dragging me along, putting my life in danger?

"It's a shame I've got to get you home. This has been some fun, hasn't it, Jimmy boy?"

"We never made it to Pascagoula," I said.

"Plans change. When the heat dies down and I'm back this way, I'll pick you up again, and we'll have even more fun."

I couldn't think any farther than the front bumper of the car we were sitting in. "What will you do now?"

"I got a guy in Jacksonville who'll give me at least a grand for a banger like this."

"Then what?"

"What you mean?"

"What'll you do after that?"

"I never know until I get there."

"That's it? Just a series of scams and near-death experiences?"

"That and some hard work at sea, yeah."

"No plan? No goals?"

"What are *your* plans and goals, smart-ass?"

"I don't know. I'm half your age."

The next twenty miles went by in silence. The car had an AM/FM radio, but neither of us reached to turn it on.

The alcohol and adrenaline had me seeing spots by the time we pulled up in front of my modest brick house. Rain fell in fat drops that exploded upon impact.

"You know what I like best about you, Jimmy boy?"

"My accuracy with a knife?"

Billy laughed and rubbed the back of his neck. "You know it! But despite all your instincts and the stuff you know, you're also aware of the shit you *don't* know yet."

The windows fogged from our breath.

"Well, my favorite nephew, I hope you had some fun."

"Aren't you going to come in and see Dad?"

"Not this time."

We shook hands in the soul grip he'd taught me, and he pulled me in for a hug.

"Next time, we'll try it without uninvited guests."

"You know it!" Guilt choked moisture from my mouth, and I coughed. It might be a year or more until Billy came back through here. I could be in college or the seminary by then.

"Aside from the peckerwoods and those two Amazons, we had a great time, didn't we?"

"Never a dull moment," I said. And then, after an awkward silence, I tacked on, "That's for sure."

"Come on, Jimmy boy, lighten up. Trust me when I say nobody at school on Monday will have a better story than yours."

"You're not worried one of my friends might report us to the authorities?"

Billy snapped his fingers and pointed at me. "No. But I like the way you think."

"What do you mean, no?"

"Most of 'em won't believe you." He spat out the window. "And those who do won't be the type to rat you out." His face brightened. "But if you tell it right, all of 'em will be entertained."

As I walked to the door, I counted the blessings I usually over-looked. I leaned low enough that the key on the chain around my neck reached the lock. I opened the door as slowly as possible. The hinges stayed quiet, and, just as I suspected, my father had fallen asleep on the couch, the television emitting the blue-and-white glow of off-air snow.

I crossed to his side, slid his eyeglasses from his face, and set them on the side table.

A surge of undefinable emotion struck me in that moment. Its nature remains mysterious to me even to this day.

I held the key against my chest and bent down to kiss his temple.

In my room, I whipped off my belt and let the knife fall to

the floor.

Standing there, surrounded by my baseball trophies, swimming medals, and merit badges, it struck me that I had achieved nothing of any real value. I couldn't accept that any longer.

My father had long planned on my becoming either a priest or a naval officer. Neither sounded exciting to me. But after walking a mile in Billy's shoes, I no longer wanted the kind of fun that could get me arrested or killed.

In that quiet moment, I jumped into the Cajun two-step a woman named Delphine had taught me at the Stateline Bar.

I danced to burn off the adrenaline coursing through me. I danced in the excitement that I'd survived an ordeal I never before would've dared to dream. I danced for the pure joy of the realization I could work as hard as my father yet find a way to be as free as my uncle. All in pursuit of a way of life that would keep me from ever having the need to look over my shoulder or to hurt another woman.

Win or lose, I was no longer headed into the mouth of Satan, but was setting out across the wild meridian as the captain of my own ship.

That's what I was born for.

Don't Stop the Carnival
Released 1998

"Intro: The Legend of Norman Paperman/Kinja"
"Public Relations"
"Calaloo"
"Grapefruit—Juicy Fruit"
"Island Fever"
"Sheila Says"
"Just an Old Truth Teller"
"Henny's Song: The Key to My Man"
"Kinja Rules"
"A Thousand Steps to Nowhere"
"It's All About the Water"
"Champagne Si, Agua No"
"Public Relations (Reprise)"
"The Handiest Frenchman in the Caribbean"
"Hippolyte's Habitat (Qui Moun' Qui)"
"Who Are We Trying to Fool?"
"Fat Person Man"
"Up on the Hill"
"Domicile"
"Funeral Dance"
"Time to Go Home"

All songs by Jimmy Buffett.

PUBLIC RELATIONS

Neil Plakcy

When Dick Jeffries was caught on camera barebacking a young male exotic dancer, I kicked into full damage control mode. It wasn't just that he was a married man and a member of the WASP establishment—he was the CEO of a company that made and marketed condoms.

As soon as Dick notified me, I flew to New York from my home on St. Thomas and took an Uber to his penthouse apartment on Central Park West. It was a bitter cold January day, and by five o'clock the sun was already setting. Was that a metaphor for the end of Dick's career, and perhaps even my own? I sure as hell hoped not.

There were bags under his eyes, his comb-over was askew, and his chin was grizzled with gray and white fuzz. His gait tottered as he led me into the living room, which had floor-to-ceiling glass windows through which I could see Central Park and the glittering towers of the East Side.

His wife had already decamped for their place in the Hamptons, and the apartment was echoingly quiet. Dick had a laptop open on a square table he'd pulled over to the leather couch, and I sat beside him. Together we looked at the *Post* article, which I had read a half-dozen times on my flight to New York.

It was fronted by a press photo of Dick I had selected to

207

minimize his double chin. We'd used Photoshop to iron out some of the creases in his face and diminish the glow from his bald spot.

The story contrasted with the picture's kindly-grandfather image. "Richard Jeffries, CEO of Custom Resources, Inc., manufacturer of the Wilde Men line of prophylactics, was videotaped Monday night having unprotected anal sex with Justin Case, an exotic dancer at Ethel's, a gay bar on the Lower East Side. Case alleges that Jeffries picked him up at the bar after Case's last performance and accompanied him to Case's apartment in Alphabet City."

My heart dropped. I had worked with Dick for a few years, and he'd had the typical bonhomie I associated with straight guys who worked in industries that dealt, however peripherally, with the fact that human beings have sexual relations.

"How did this get out?" I asked.

"Little bastard posted it on YouTube and then pushed it on Twitter. I don't know why. I tipped him a hundred bucks at the bar and gave him another two hundred when I left his apartment."

"Did he give you any indication that he knew who you were?"

"I wouldn't have fucked him if he had," Dick said harshly.

The fact that Dick was married to a woman was troubling. But hey, gay and bisexual men get dragged out of the closet all the time these days, and a good PR man can put the right spin on that. Offer apologies to those he's hurt, vow to live an honest life, join the board of a prominent LGBT organization.

The bigger problem was that Dick was the CEO of a company that promoted smart sex, yet he was caught on camera barebacking. If the CEO himself doesn't use the product, that could damage the brand, perhaps irreparably.

"I have a board meeting scheduled for tomorrow morning, Norman. Probably can my ass, unless you can do something for me pronto."

He picked up a martini glass from the white marble table in front of him. I could tell he was on his third or fourth by then.

"Let's start with the basics," I said. "Are you gay, bisexual, gender fluid?"

"What the fuck?"

"We need to frame this situation, and that's going to take some soul-searching from you. If you're gay, we go one way. If you're bisexual, we go another."

"Can't we say this was a one-time mistake?"

I stared at him.

He met my eyes for a minute, then looked down at his martini. "This wasn't my first rodeo, all right?"

He got up and went into the kitchen. "Jesus, this is hard to say," he said, when he returned with another martini. He took a deep breath. "I'm gay."

I lifted my own martini. "Welcome to the club," I said.

I often say that my love for the Caribbean began because I was born on an island—Manhattan. From the time I was old enough to ride the subway on my own, I spent my weekends in darkened theaters and dreamed of a career on the Great White Way, but the world had other plans for me.

After a career in trade publication in the pharmaceutical industry, I launched my own PR agency. I hustled for headlines, grappled for gossip, and worked the press for a mention or two. I was liberal with concert tickets and seats in tiny theaters in the Village and Tribeca. But my bread and butter came from companies like Custom Resources.

All those years of good living—martinis at lunch, Porterhouse steaks for dinner—added up to a minor heart attack. I came out of the closet, sold my condo, moved to St. Thomas, and I've never been happier. Thanks to modern technology, I continue to work for a few solid clients, including Custom Resources. But if I couldn't get Dick out of this jam, my tropical caper might go down the drain.

* * *

"Repeat after me," I told him. "Because of my inner conflict about my sexual orientation, I acted in a manner that doesn't reflect the man I am."

He gaped at me.

"Go on, say it."

He did, stumbling over a couple of words.

I continued. "After a period of soul-searching I have realized that, in order to live my life fully and best serve the staff and customers of Custom Resources, I need to acknowledge that I'm a gay man. I apologize to anyone I've hurt."

"You want me to say that?" he demanded.

"Or something like it. Now for the really tough question: Why the fuck didn't you use a condom?"

"I didn't have one with me."

"Dick, you run a company that *makes* them, for Christ's sake. Why don't you carry a half dozen of them in your pocket or your briefcase?"

When I was a kid, we had a beagle puppy, and whenever he peed on the floor or chewed something up, he had the most baleful expression. Dick looked like that.

"Don't tell me you don't believe in them," I said.

"There's nothing like skin-to-skin contact. You must know that."

"I also know I don't want to become H-I-V positive or wind up with gonorrhea or syphilis." I held up my hand. "And don't even *tell* me he looked clean, or I'll think you're too stupid to defend."

His mouth opened and closed.

"I need to think about this," I said. "Give me a minute."

I closed my eyes and ran through scenarios. There was no way I was letting Dick admit that he didn't use condoms regularly. That would cost him his job, if he hadn't lost it already, and tank sales of the Wilde Men line.

We'd have to go with 'the heat of the moment.'

"You were taken advantage of," I said. "I'm not saying you weren't at fault. You picked up a stranger and you didn't use a condom. But it's possible he came after you for a reason."

"Why?"

"There are at least nine other brands that command a share of the condom market," I said. "This could have been a way to discredit you and Wilde Men."

"You think somebody from one of my competitors convinced this kid to videotape me barebacking? You've always been Numero Uno at coming up with out-of-the-box ideas, Norman, but that's pretty wild, even for you."

There was a rap on the apartment door.

"Expecting someone?"

Dick shook his head. "Must be neighbors. I'll get rid of them."

He opened the door to a pair of uniformed police officers flanking a man in a dark suit. "Richard Jeffries?" the suited man asked.

"That's me."

"You're under arrest for the murder of Justin Chekowksi, also known as Justin Case."

Dick's arrest meant I needed a new strategy to deal with the media. I called Ray Castiglione, the director of marketing for the Wilde Men line, and arranged to meet him right away at CR's Park Avenue office.

Ray was a thirty-something former college jock, with square shoulders and a solid handshake. He led me into one of the small conference rooms. "Hell of a thing," he said, as we sat down. "Bad enough for Dick to get caught screwing around, but even worse that he wasn't using our product."

"I haven't watched the video closely," I said. "Is it clear he was barebacking?"

Ray shuddered. "I got a much closer look at the boss's dick

than I ever wanted. Yeah, he was condom-free."

"For now, I suggest a solid 'no comment' from the company."
I took a breath. "I met with Dick at his apartment before I came
here. Our conversation was interrupted, though, by New York's
finest."

Ray's mouth gaped open. "He was arrested? For public inde-
cency?"

"For murder. Justin Case is dead."

"Oh, shit!"

"No kidding. I understand you have a board meeting tomorrow. If Dick isn't immediately fired, he'll certainly be put on a
leave of absence. We need a press release ready for either
eventuality."

We drafted two statements for Susan Black, Wilde Men's
brand manager, she approved them, and I Ubered to my hotel
and went online.

I was impressed at the speed with which the *Post* had put
together a follow-up article. Justin Case was twenty-two, a native
of Scranton, where he had been a drama-club standout, star of
his senior-year production of *Grease.* He had been a finalist for
the Jimmy Award for students in high school musical theater, a
young man his drama coach said had "great promise."

He had moved to New York City at nineteen with hopes of
getting a job on or off Broadway, but quickly turned to dancing
in gay bars to pay the bills while waiting for his big break. He
nearly scored a role in the chorus of *Dear Evan Hansen,* but the
director caught him on the bar at Ethel's, and that put the kibosh
on his chance at a family friendly job.

I'd run across a lot of kids like Justin. Talented singers and
dancers in their small hometowns, they think they have what it
takes to succeed in the big city. Some return home in defeat,
others find alternative careers, too many succumb to the lure of
drugs or the easy money of the sex trade.

At nine o'clock, I headed over to Ethel's to see what else I
could learn about Justin Case. I had been a regular there for a

while, after I came out of the closet. I wasn't comfortable in leather, didn't want to dance shirtless, and hated house music, so Ethel's—which was one of the few old-fashioned gay bars left in the city—worked for me. It skewed to an older crowd, men in their forties and fifties who had cash to share with cute guys in bikini briefs. The décor was a mix of old theatrical posters of Ethel Merman in *Gypsy* and *Annie Get Your Gun*, and posters and Christmas ornaments in the shape of sexy shirtless guys with fishy tails.

If you pass the piano bar and turn right, you enter a darker room lit by spotlights on the catwalk. That was where Justin had worked. But I didn't head back there right away; instead, I stopped at the front bar to talk to Manil, the young Sri Lankan bartender.

He recognized me, even though I hadn't been there for months. Boozing and schmoozing, that's what I do—and I tip well, too. I ordered a cosmopolitan and took a seat. "You knew Justin well?" I asked, when Manil brought me my drink.

He shrugged. "Enough to know he was nowhere near as sweet and innocent as he played on stage."

That was interesting news. "How so? Did he pick up older men regularly?"

Manil nodded. His coffee-colored skin glowed in the light. "The more married, the better. And that guy from the condom company? He wasn't the first one Justin tried to screw over."

I picked up my cosmo and sipped.

"Two weeks ago, a businessman came in, all pissed off. He said Justin had the back-room bartender pad his tab with extra charges. A thousand bucks' worth."

"And did he?"

Manil shrugged. "There was a difference of opinion about that. The bartender got fired, the manager reversed the businessman's charges, and Justin skated."

"You ever hear of him videotaping anyone else?"

"He bragged about it. Check his YouTube channel."

"Anyone ever complain?"

"Not that I heard." Manil went off to serve other customers, and I sipped my drink.

I was tempted to hang around, watch the dancers, fill their jockstraps with singles and fives, and lose myself in a world I'd left behind when I moved to St. Thomas. But I was working for Dick, and I needed a clear head.

I went around the corner to a Belgian restaurant I loved, ordered a bowl of mussels. Sipping a Kriek Boon, I considered the situation. I had spoken with my client and his staff and written the necessary press releases. Technically, my work was done. I could catch the next flight back to St. Thomas and take care of any necessary follow-up by Skype.

But I sympathized with Dick. I had come out of the closet voluntarily, but it had still been a tough road, and I appreciated the kindnesses my friends had showed me. I wanted to pay that forward by continuing to help Dick Jeffries.

Besides, something was nagging at me. Why had Justin taped his encounters? For blackmail? Had Dick refused to pay? That would explain why the video had been released.

But why kill Justin after the tape had already gone viral? In a fit of anger? That meant Dick would have had to track Justin down and arrange a way to take his life. But I couldn't see him as a cold-blooded killer.

I finished my dinner and asked for the check, and my phone rang. I was surprised to recognize Dick's number. "They let me go," he said. "Can you come back over here?"

It was nearly eleven, but Dick and Custom Resources paid a big chunk of the money that allowed me to live my life of sunshine and sea air, so I said sure and Ubered over there.

"The kid was killed Tuesday night," Dick told me, "between eight o'clock and eleven. I was at Sardi's all that time, entertaining a couple of retailers from the Midwest. My tab was stamped at eleven-forty, and the two guys I was with and the waiter all corroborate my story."

"Did Justin contact you after you left his apartment?" I asked.

"If you mean did he try to bribe me to keep the video out of the news, the answer is no. I didn't know his last name when I walked out of that hole in the wall where he lived. I didn't have his phone number or any other way to get hold of him. He didn't contact me, and I didn't contact him."

"Then why did he release the video? Was he angry? Did you hurt him?"

"I might have slapped his butt a couple of times, but that's it." He got up. "You want a martini?"

"I'll pass," I said. "And I think you should, too. You have a board meeting tomorrow morning. I'm going back to my hotel, but I'm going to stick around for a day or two, in case you need anything else."

"Thanks, Norman."

When I stood up, he embraced me in an awkward one-armed hug, but it was time for him to get accustomed to being warm with other gay men, so I pulled him in tighter. Though he might have been Justin Case's type, he wasn't mine, and there was nothing more than friendship in our embrace.

"I'm here for you, Dick. Call me if you need anything."

"I appreciate it, Norman. I guess I'll take a couple of pills and see if I can get some sleep."

Thursday morning, I woke with a renewed desire to do what I could to help Dick Jeffries. The police had cleared him of Justin's murder, but as long as the case remained open there would be speculation about him, and I wanted him to be able to move forward.

I looked at my notes. I wanted to understand why Justin had targeted Dick, why he'd uploaded the video, and why he'd been killed.

I returned to my initial suspicion of corporate espionage. Suppose someone Dick had fucked in the past knew he didn't use his own company's condoms, and that information had trickled down to one of Wilde Men's competitors?

When I began working for Custom Resources, I researched their competition. Now I found that folder on my laptop and read through it.

Ten companies dominated the condom market worldwide: Custom Resources was number three after Durex and Trojan, which were too big to obtain much of any benefit from the destruction of the Wilde Men line.

I studied the rest of the top ten, but none was headquartered in New York. No, I couldn't come up with any viable suspects that way.

Manil had told me Justin had a YouTube channel, so I searched for it and found other videos similar to the one with Dick. Justin's targets were fleshy blond middle-aged men who wore wedding rings. Each had a blustery behavior in the bedroom, pushing Justin around, slapping him, intent only on his own pleasure, not Justin's.

On instinct, I went back to the *Post's* profile. Justin was the son of Marie and the late Donald Chekowksi, and I looked up Donald's obituary. There was a photo of him, and, just as I would have guessed, he was a broad-shouldered blond man who bore a general physical resemblance to Dick Jeffries and the other targets.

That had to mean something. Had Donald abused Justin as a kid? Was this Justin's way of getting back at his father? If necessary, I could push the angle that Justin was working out his anger toward his father with a bunch of similar men, which would paint a more sympathetic picture of Dick Jeffries.

I had picked up a bar rag called *Loisaida Men* at Ethel's the night before, and I flipped through it. The purpose of such publications is to advertise gay bars and companies that serve the community, and the ads are interspersed with photos of recent local events: a Sunday T-dance, a Pig Night, a drag-queen revue. There was a full-page ad for Wilde Men condoms, then a series of photos from a day-spa promotion at Ethel's. Lots of customers getting manicures and pedicures and facials from scantily clad hunks.

One photo showed a man much younger than Dick Jeffries but of the same mold: broad-shouldered, sandy blond hair, five-o'clock shadow. Had he been one of Justin's victims, too? No, I realized, he wasn't a customer, he was one of the bartenders. The photo caption identified him only as Keith.

My phone rang.

"Board met this morning," Dick said. "I'm on a temporary leave of absence to work out my 'personal issues.'" I could hear the air quotes. "You busy? I could use some company."

"I'm on my way," I said.

When I got there, Dick was sober, dressed in the conservative business suit he'd worn to the board meeting. His tie was loosened, the top button of his dress shirt open.

"I've been doing some research on Justin," I said. "Did he ever say you reminded him of his father?"

"He did. You can't hear it in the video, but he asked if he could call me daddy."

That explained why Justin had chosen him.

"Did the cops think he knew who you were?"

Dick frowned. "My wife once gave me a monogramed business-card holder. The police had it and asked where Justin had gotten it. I said it must have fallen out of my pocket."

"So he *did* know who you were."

"But why destroy my life?" Dick's voice was strangled. "He didn't even *know* me."

"It had nothing to do with you," I explained. "You look like his father, and he had issues there he needed to work out."

"You think maybe one of the men in one of the other videos killed him?"

"I'm going to suggest that possibility to the police. You ever run across a bartender at Ethel's named Keith?"

"Big, dumb-looking blond?"

I nodded.

"Yeah, he got fired last week for cheating a customer."

Manil had said the fired bartender and Justin had worked a scam together. "Do you know Keith's last name?"

"Bryan. I remember because of Brian Keith, you know, the actor? I always had kind of a crush on him."

I was glad to see Dick opening up. He'd been gay a long time before Justin Case videotaped him.

I began making connections. Keith the bartender had been fired for cheating customers, and Justin had gotten away without penalty. That gave Keith a reason to be angry with Justin.

Dick leaned back. "Justin said Keith lived down the street from him in Alphabet City. They used to walk to work together."

Another interesting detail.

"Did the cops tell you where they found Justin's body?"

"Tompkins Square Park, not far from his apartment. They think he was on his way to work."

Justin and Keith lived near each other and often walked to work together, so Keith would have known that Justin cut through that park on his way to Ethel's.

Dick excused himself, and I opened my laptop and initialized a program that cross-referenced names, cell phone numbers and addresses. I use it occasionally when I need a journalist's private cell number.

I plugged in "Keith Brian" and "New York" and got nothing. But when I switched "Brian" to "Bryan," I got the hit I needed.

"I've got to run an errand," I called, and headed out the door.

Locals often call Avenue C "Loisaida Avenue," after the Span-ish-inflected pronunciation of "Lower East Side." The address I had was a five-story walk-up with fire escapes lining the front of the building, sandwiched between a dry cleaner and a

Chinese takeout.

I surveyed the list of residents and found that "Bryan" was in 5F. A girl with a long blue braid slipped out, and I grabbed the door before it could click shut.

The climb to the fifth floor winded me. What the hell I was *doing* there? Why hadn't I called the cops?

Because all I had was a suspicion, and who knew if they'd follow up? Despite the initial publicity surrounding the murder, Justin Case was a member of the underclass—a poor young guy who showed off his body for money and committed the cardinal sin of taping a member of the upper class while having sex. He wasn't going to win any awards for Man of the Year, and his murder would probably be quickly forgotten.

I wanted justice for Justin—and for Dick Jeffries, who'd been dragged through the sewer because of one mistake.

When my breathing was regular again, I knocked on the door.

The guy who opened it matched the photos from Ethel's. Five-nine, wearing a tank top that clung to his chest and exposed his guns, skinny jeans and lace-up work boots. "I'm on my way out," he said. "What do you want?"

"I want to talk about Justin Case."

"You better come in, then."

The studio apartment had a single window that looked out at Avenue C. There was a double bed along one wall, a galley kitchen on the other. The place smelled like fried rice and marijuana.

"What about Justin?" he demanded.

"I know he threw you under the bus at Ethel's," I said. "Sucks that *he* didn't get canned, too."

He nodded. "He'd pick out a mark he thought was married or on an expense account. He'd order all these fancy drinks, and I'd run two parallel charges on the guy's card, one to an L-L-C my brother set up for me. I'd split the second tab with Justin, and the guy wouldn't see the charge until he got his bill at the end of the month. Justin figured he wouldn't want his wife or his boss to know where he'd been, so he wouldn't complain."

219

"Clever."

"It worked for a couple of months. But then this one mark came back, bitching about his bill, and Justin put it all on me."

"Ouch."

"Cost me my job. I had my eye on the little bastard after that." He looked at me, and something in his eyes hardened. "Are you some kind of cop?"

He was bigger, younger and stronger than I was, and I realized I'd made a stupid move coming to his apartment alone. I backed away, but he grabbed my arm. "I recognize you. You come to Ethel's sometimes. You never tip the dancers, and you never leave with anyone. You *must* be a cop."

"I'm not," I said. "But I figured out you followed Justin from his apartment to Tompkins Square Park and killed him, and I've left a message for the detective investigating the case."

"What do you want?"

My heart raced. "I think you're hella sexy," I said. "Maybe we can set up a deal: I don't tell the cops what I know, and you fuck me when I need it."

He looked at me with disgust. "Old guy like you? No way."

I lunged for the door and was out in the hall before he could react. I zoomed down the stairs like there was a rocket under my ass, with Keith Bryan close behind me.

On Avenue C, a Toyota SUV pulled to the curb. The back door popped open, and Dick Jeffries yelled "Get in!" as Keith grabbed for the door.

The driver took off.

"Precinct headquarters on West 20th," Dick told him.

It took me a full minute to catch my breath. "How did you know where I was?"

"I ran after you." Dick looked embarrassed. "I thought maybe I did something stupid and needed to apologize. The doorman told me he heard you give your Uber driver an address on Avenue C, and I wanted to help."

I laughed. "Funny, I thought *I* was helping *you*."

* * *

Dick took charge at the police station, asking for the detective he'd spoken with the day before. I gave a full statement, and the detective chastised me for interfering with an open investigation. "This Brian Keith is probably in the wind by now," he grumbled.

"Keith Bryan," I said.

He glared at me.

Dick took me to Sardi's for a celebratory lunch, and by the time we were finished we were both half-drunk and very happy. He invited me up to his apartment afterward, but I declined.

"Can't blame a guy for trying," he said.

I stayed in New York for an extra day, meeting with a couple of clients I don't see very often. By the time I returned to St. Thomas, Keith had been arrested, Dick had been cleared of the murder, and I'd orchestrated the start of his coming-out process.

Custom Resources went through some corporate restructuring. Susan Black was promoted to CEO, and Dick took a step down to manage the Wilde Men line. His new credentials as an openly gay man who could testify to the dangers involved in not using a condom gave him an interesting platform, and I looked forward to working with him in the future.

In the end, it's all public relations: Who's screwing who? Justin Case and Dick Jeffries had gotten screwed in different ways, but a good PR man knows how to put a spin on almost anything.

Beach House on the Moon
Released 1999

"Beach House on the Moon"
"Permanent Reminder of a Temporary Feeling"
"Waiting for the Next Explosion"
"Pacing the Cage"
"You Call It Jogging"
"Flesh and Bone"
"I Will Play For Gumbo"
"Math Suks"
"Spending Money"
"Semi-True Story"
"Lucky Stars"
"I Don't Know and I Don't Care"
"Oysters and Pearls"

"Beach House on the Moon," "Permanent Reminder of a
Temporary Feeling," "Waiting for the Next Explosion," and
"I Will Play For Gumbo" are by Jimmy Buffett,
"Pacing the Cage" is by Bruce Cockburn, "You Call It Jogging" is by John D.
Loudermilk, "Semi-True Story" is by Mac McAnally,
and "Lucky Stars" is by Roger Guth and Peter Mayer.
All other songs were written by Jimmy in collaboration with other writers:
"Flesh and Bone" (with Mac McAnally and Michael Utley),
"Math Suks" (with Roger Guth and Peter Mayer),
"Spending Money" and "Oysters and Pearls" (both with Mac McAnally),
and "I Don't Know and I Don't Care" (with Jim Mayer).

SPENDING MONEY

John M. Floyd

At half past eleven on Friday morning, Jack Elkins and his date hurried through a misty rain to the door of his favorite café on the town square. Once inside, the young lady headed for the restroom to repair her hair and makeup while he took a seat at one of the window booths and looked out at the tree-lined street. They'd made it just in time—the drizzle was becoming a downpour.

A moment later, waitress Ruthie Woods appeared at his table and dropped two lunch menus in front of him. Ruthie was one of those constants in an ever-changing world. Jack had known her at least ten years, and she didn't look as if she'd aged a day. Even her hairstyle was still the same. With a glance toward the ladies' room, she said, "Who is she this time?"

"None of your business," he said, grinning.

Ruthie grinned back, then gave him a look. "Why aren't you at work?"

That was another thing that never changed. Ruthie was always checking on him. "It's the day after Thanksgiving—nobody's working but you," he said. "Besides, it's raining."

She cocked her head and studied him a moment. "The job didn't pan out. Right?"

He let out a sigh. "Right."

"In other words, you got fired."

"Yeah, I think those are the words."

"Good God, Jack—how do you get fired after four days?"

"They found out I'd never sold insurance before."

"You told them you had?"

"Why not?" he said. "How much experience do you need to sell a life-insurance policy? Anyhow, they found out I didn't know what an incontestability clause was, and they canned me."

She rolled her eyes. "How *rude*."

"Don't make fun of me," he grumbled. "It's their loss."

"Sure it is." Ruthie dug a full bottle of ketchup from somewhere in the giant pocket of her apron and plunked it down on the table beside the salt and pepper shakers. "You know your trouble, Jack Elkins? You got no financial conscience. You don't worry about where your money comes from *or* where it goes."

"Hey, I've got money to burn," he said.

She sighed, and he saw her face soften. Outside, cars splashed through the street and pedestrians lurched along beneath wind-whipped umbrellas. "Look," she said, "if worse comes to worst—if you really need some cash, or at least some change in your pocket—we can always use another dishwasher."

"Any experience required?" Jack asked.

She grinned again.

"Don't worry," he said. "I got another job lined up. What makes me mad, though, is that after I got sacked at the insurance company, the boss called me an idiot. Can you believe that?"

"You *are* an idiot, Jack. That's why you can't keep a job. Or a girlfriend." She shot another look toward the restrooms. "Where'd you meet this one?"

"Do you know her?"

"No. She looks familiar, though."

"I met her at the grocery store last night. She helped me find the almond M&Ms."

"Oh, good—at least you're eating right."

A sudden gust of wind rattled the rain-streaked windowpane

beside the table. Both of them turned to look at it.

After a pause, Jack said, his eyes on the window, "I really like her, Ruthie. Who knows, she might be the one."

She snorted. "Don't count on it, kid. You'll probably lie to her, too, before the night's out, and that'll be the end of that."

He gave her a glum look. "Thanks for the encouragement."

"You want encouragement, buy a Zig Ziglar tape. You want advice, here it is: You can't get by in this world looking good and being funny, Jack. That's not enough. People respect honesty. Actually, they *ex*pect honesty. Just tell the truth for a change."

"And if I do, I won't be an idiot?" he asked.

They heard the restroom door open and shut, and Jack saw his date, Holly Cunningham, heading in their direction.

"You'll still be an idiot," Ruthie said, turning to leave. "But maybe she won't find out."

Holly smiled at Ruthie as they passed each other, then took a seat across from Jack and picked up her menu. "What do you suggest?" she asked him.

"The Thanksgiving special," he said. "Turkey with oyster dressing. But everything's good here."

"I'll be the judge of that." She looked up at him, smiling, and then squinted. "What's the matter?"

"Just thinking. How much experience you think it'd take to write an insurance policy?"

"What?"

"Nothing."

Holly studied his face. "You're a strange guy, Jack Elkins. And since I only know you from the candy aisle at Kroger, maybe I better be careful of you."

"Maybe you better." Now both of them were smiling. "Thanks for accepting my invitation to lunch, by the way."

"My pleasure. I'm just glad you didn't plan a picnic." As if to emphasize that thought, thunder crashed outside the window, and she turned to watch the storm. The sidewalk, less than six feet from where they sat, looked like a swift, roaring river.

"I saw an ark go by, while you were in the ladies'," he said.

"I'm not surprised."

Over Holly's shoulder, Jack saw Ruthie hold up an order pad and raise a questioning eyebrow, but he ignored her. He didn't want to be interrupted right now. After a minute or so, he said, "How is it I haven't seen you around town before?"

She shrugged. "I travel a lot." She lowered her menu and focused on him. "Are we at the point where we tell each other what we do for a living?"

"I guess so," he said.

"Okay, then: I'm an aerobics instructor. I teach classes out of town the first three days of every week."

No wonder she looks so good, Jack thought. He hoped she wouldn't suggest, as Ruthie often did, that he try to get in shape himself. "Impressive," he said, as another roll of thunder shook the building.

"Not really. It's just fun. Not a world-changing career, but satisfying."

"Is it something you always wanted to do?"

"No. But I graduated in Phys. Ed. at the college here and worked at a gym to pay my way through, so..."

"I went to school here, too," Jack said.

"Really? What was your major?"

He started to lie, then remembered what Ruthie had said. "Liberal Arts," he answered.

"And what do you do now?"

I look good and I'm funny, Jack thought. But what he said was, "Different things." Which, again, was true. He didn't add that none of those things was in any way interesting, or that he hadn't actually *finished* college. But that wasn't exactly lying. "Where'd you work?" he asked.

"While I was in school? Fitness Corner, on East Raleigh."

"Me, too."

Holly's eyebrows lifted. "You worked at Fitness Corner?"

He smiled. "No, I mean I also had to work to pay my tuition."

"Where?"

"The pool hall on campus." What he didn't say was that he hadn't been on the payroll. He'd hustled games there for a year before the sad crash-and-burn of his academic career. Just for spending money, mostly, but still. "That, and a few innovative things."

"Innovative?" she said.

Jack decided to take a chance. She seemed broadminded, this Holly Cunningham, and maybe a little mischievous. So far, he'd been truthful—well, at least not *un*truthful—so why not appeal to her adventurous side? He hoped she had one.

He took a deep breath, chose his words carefully, and told her a story he'd never told anyone before. A story he hadn't even thought about for years.

"Freshman year," he began, "I lived in a ten-story dorm. Bowden Hall. I was always broke, like a lot of my classmates, and I got used to going downstairs to the basement every night and grabbing a snack from one of the candy machines there. I still remember the name on those machines: Birdwell Vending. Anyhow, one night I made a discovery. It was an accident, really. I bought a candy bar and then tried to buy another one, and the machine wouldn't give it to me. It took me a while to understand why—but it was about two in the morning and I was the only one there, so I had plenty of time, and I finally figured it out."

Holly frowned. "Figured what out?"

"How to make rainy days"—he pointed to the window—"a little less bleak."

The frown deepened. "What are you talking about?"

Patiently, he said, "I figured out how to get myself some spending money."

"What? From where?"

"From the vending machines." He gave her his best, most mysterious, grin. "What happened was, I got my first candy bar by pulling out the plunger directly underneath my selection—it was maybe four inches long, with a big red button on the end to hold onto. When I pulled it, my snack dropped into the hopper and I could reach in and get it out. But when I turned loose of the plunger and let it slide back into the machine, well, for some reason it didn't go all the way in. It stopped about half an inch short of re-seating. And since it didn't seat properly, when I yanked a different plunger for a different selection, nothing happened. I banged on the machine and rocked it back and forth and cussed a blue streak, but no dice. I lost my money for that second candy bar—a Butterfinger, I think it was."

Holly sat there, an odd look on her face, listening and waiting.

"I finally solved the problem, though. I fiddled around with that first plunger, and it eased back into the machine and seated itself the way it should've in the first place—and when that happened, all was well. I could go ahead and buy other snacks. Most important, though, when I reseated the plunger, I hit the coin-return button and got back the money I'd lost on my second selection."

"So?" Holly asked. "You got back your fifty cents, or whatever. Right?"

"Seventy-five cents. But you're missing the point. Once I figured out what was going on, I started going down to the vending machines in the basements of all the dorms every night around seven or eight o'clock—eight dorms, thirty-two machines—and rigging one of the plungers on each machine so it didn't quite go all the way back in. I'd just wedge a little folded piece of paper in there underneath the head of the button, and I'd always choose a plunger underneath a selection that wasn't all that popular— pork skins, sunflower seeds, something like that, something I figured nobody'd try. Then, about four in the morning, I'd go back again, take out the piece of paper, reseat the plunger, hit the coin-return button, and out would flow all the quarters and dimes and nickels that had been put in for candies that never got dispensed. I'd get four or five bucks out of each machine, which amounted to maybe a hundred dollars a night, sometimes more. Now and then, somebody would figure it out like I had and fix it, but that was rare. I did a pretty good business for five months or so. I had money to burn."

Jack paused, feeling almost as much pride in his scam now as he'd felt all those years ago. From the corner of his eye he noticed that the wind had died down and the pounding rain had almost stopped. Off to the west, the sky was clearing.

"What do you think of that?" he asked Holly. "My story, not the weather."

She sat there for several seconds, looking at him.

Jack broke the silence with a thought that had only now occurred to him. "You know, I never see those Birdwell machines anymore. Haven't seen 'em in a long time."

Finally, Holly spoke. "That's because the company went out of business," she said, her voice strange.

"They did?"

She fixed him with a dark stare. "Probably because of people like you."

He felt his face heat up. "Wait a minute. It's not like I robbed an armored car or a time-locked vault. They were vending machines."

She picked up her purse. "It doesn't matter. That was a terrible thing you did. You thought it was some kind of game, but you were wrong. You *stole*, Jack. Robbing a bank would have meant more money, that's the only difference."

Jack frowned. "You're not going to report me, are you? I mean, that was *years* ago."

Her cheeks were flushed, her eyes hard as flint. "No, I won't report you. But I'm sure as hell not having lunch with you." She slid out of the booth and glared down at him. "You're an idiot, you know that?"

As she stormed off, Ruthie came back to the booth, and the two of them watched Holly push through the front door and march away down the street, dodging rain puddles and still-dripping tree branches.

"What in the world did you say to her?"

231

Jack stayed quiet awhile, trying to process all this. At last he said, "The truth. And remember what you said, about me being an idiot?"

"Yeah?"

"She found out."

Ruthie didn't reply to that, but she seemed unsurprised.

After a moment, Jack dug around in his pocket and looked up at her. "You got any change?"

"Why? We don't have a pay phone anymore."

"I don't want to make a call, Ruthie, and I don't want lunch. I want a Three Musketeers. From that big candy machine in the back."

"Don't have that anymore, either, haven't had it for years. The company that made 'em—Birdwell Vending—went under."

He felt his shoulders slump. "I heard about that," he said. "I liked those machines."

Ruthie nodded toward the doorway. "That's what you should've said to your date." "What?"

"I finally remembered who she was. Holly Cunningham, right?"

"Yeah," he said. "Why?"

"Her uncle's Harlan Birdwell."

"You mean—"

"The guy who owned the vending company."

Jack gulped. "You're kidding."

"Nope."

He rubbed his eyes. "I got news for you, Ruthie. Honesty might *not* always be the best policy."

A long silence passed. Ruthie picked up the menus, wiped the table, and watched him stare out the window at the traffic. The sun, which had come out again, glinted off chrome and windshields. Finally, she said, "What're you thinking?"

He looked up. "Remember what you said about me needing spending money?"

"Sure, what about it?"

He let out a long breath. "How much do you pay your dishwashers?"

Ruthie grinned. "I thought you already had a new job lined up."

"I lied," he said.

Songs From St. Somewhere
Released 2013

"Somethin' 'Bout a Boat"
"Einstein Was a Surfer"
"Earl's Dead—Cadillac For Sale"
"Too Drunk to Karaoke"
"Serpentine"
"Useless But Important Information"
"I Want to Go Back to Cartagena"
"Soufully"
"Rue de la Guitare"
"I'm No Russian"
"Tides"
"The Rocket That Grandpa Rode"
"I Wave Bye Bye"
"Colour of the Sun"
"Oldest Surfer on the Beach"
"I Want to Go Back to Cartagena" (Spanish version)

"Earl's Dead—Cadillac For Sale," "Rue de la Guitare,"
and "I'm No Russian" are by Jimmy Buffett.
"Somethin' 'Bout a Boat" is by Django Walker, Dave Berg, Patrick Davis,
Jedd Hughes, James Otto, and Eric Paslay,
"Soulfully" is by Will Kimbrough, "I Wave Bye Bye" is by Jesse Winchester,
and "Oldest Surfer on the Beach" is by Mark Knopfler.
All other songs were written by Jimmy in collaboration with other writers:
"Einstein Was a Surfer," "Serpentine," and
"Useless But Important Information" (with Mac McAnally),
"Too Drunk to Karaoke" (with McAnally, Shawn Camp,
and Pat McLaughlin),
"I Want to Go Back to Cartagena" (both versions with Peter Mayer,
Roger Guth, and Kimbrough),
"Tides" (with Guth), "The Rocket That Grandpa Rode" (with McAnally,
Kimbrough, Mayer, and Guth),
and "Colour of the Sun" (with McAnally, Mayer, and Guth).

EINSTEIN WAS A SURFER

M.E. Browning

Lesson One: Don't Be a Kook

Rincon Point Park didn't open until six, but already members of the dawn patrol had claimed their spots in the parking lot. Most kept to themselves, suiting up, taking a last sip of coffee, pulling their surfboards off racks, out of truck beds, eager to beat the sun to the water and catch a wave before heading to their soul-sucking day jobs.

One couple held hands and jaw-jacked in the shadows, waiting for the December sun to gain a bit more elevation. Cars screamed along the nearby 101 freeway. Another half hour, and congestion would dull the roar to a relentless drone.

Einstein backed his van into a parking spot. Living near the ocean had left his windshield rimed with salt, and he peered through it, imagining the waves that crashed on the other side of the multi-million-dollar homes that squatted on the point, hidden behind a screen of eucalyptus, oleander, and fence. A rocky beach stretched between the enclave and ocean, strewn with the kind of cobblestones he and his old cycling buddies had called baby heads.

But it was the waves, not the beach, that drew people to Rincon. Perfectly formed, they lapped and crashed and tumbled against the beach. Those waves wielded power, inspired people to do things they'd never thought possible, changed lives—not always for good.

He'd first surfed Rincon when he was a nine-year-old kook, a newbie who knew nothing of the sport or the etiquette that went with it. When he turned sixteen, he bought a piece-of-shit Corolla that cost less than his board. Every school day, if the tide was right, he'd defy his father and dial a nine-seven-six number for an up-to-the-minute surf report. If it looked even marginal, he'd bungee his board to the roof and go. If the waves were six feet and glassy, there was a good chance he'd ditch class and stay out all morning.

That was the Eighties. Back then, he'd had to park along the freeway shoulder, grab his board and make a mad dash across four lanes of traffic. Today there were dedicated parking lots and apps—apps for weather, for wind, for waves, for tides, for damn near anything one needed, surf-related or not.

One of his former surfing students, a gal he hadn't seen in a while, crossed the lot carrying a shortboard. He rolled down the window of his van. Cold morning air flooded the cab with a tang so briny he could taste it. He tapped the horn.

Beth squinted through the gathering light, broke into a smile, and veered toward the van. "Hey, Einstein! New wheels?"

"You need to get out more. The van's a year old, now."

"New boyfriend. You know how it is."

"Why isn't he here? Don't tell me he doesn't surf. It's okay with me if he's ugly, but he better surf."

Beth balanced the bottom of her board on her foot and ran her free hand through her hair. The same sun-bleached hair Einstein had sported as a teen, back when he was still known as Peter. "Anyway, the lineup lately's been nothing but kooks."

"So teach them a lesson."

She laughed. "There you go again. Always with the lessons."

"I seem to remember schooling *you* a couple times," he said. "We're all kooks when we start."

"Maybe so, but not like this. These guys are so clueless they're dangerous." Her face reddened. "Hey, man, no disrespect."

"None taken."

"You gonna hang?"

Einstein held up his laptop. "I've got some work to do."

Beth worked her thumb back and forth across her surfboard leash like it was a rosary. When she spoke, her voice was soft. "You know, that asshole still has the balls to show up here, three or four times a week. He's toting a new longboard that's every bit as ridiculous as his first one."

"Yeah, I know." The board in question was a rad Vintage Buzzy Trent model balsawood 1964 Pipeliner by Dick Brewer. The last one to come up at auction had gone for a cool eighteen grand. It wasn't the board that was ridiculous, it was the rider. "I say hello, every time I see him, just to piss him off."

"*He's* someone I'd like to school," Beth said.

Einstein fired up his laptop. "He'll get his."

Lesson Two: Give Respect to Get Respect

It was nine o'clock when Einstein closed his laptop, stowed it on the passenger seat, and merged onto the 101 north. He was a Ventura native, and most everything in his life required traveling north. For years, it was surfing Rincon. Then for a while, he went farther afield, traveling the world, chasing waves. He had earned the nickname Einstein on the pro circuit for his ability to read the waves. He was good—really good—but not quite great. No biggie. He'd had a hell of a lot of fun along the way.

Then it was home again, broke, but in love with a Goleta girl. After that, life caught up. He earned a scholarship to UCSB—a school chosen solely for its proximity to surf—then got a job as a systems administrator for a financial services group in Carpinteria. Through it all, he surfed the Rincon and shared his knowledge with the kooks who showed up eager to learn how to catch a wave.

Today he drove north to Santa Barbara, and before he knew it, he was negotiating the city's narrow streets. He wove his way toward the towering courthouse, his destination one of the law offices that had sprung up like toadstools in its shadow. Parking in Santa Barbara was hellish at the best of times, and it took two loops before a space opened up on Anacapa.

With the click of the remote, the side door rolled open, the hydraulics lowered the van slightly, and the ramp unfolded. He unlocked the wheels of his chair and spun toward the door. The wheelchair lurched slightly where the ramp hinged with the van, and then again when he rolled over the lip at the sidewalk. Another remote click reversed the sequence, and he chirped the lock.

The Santa Barbara Courthouse consumed an entire block of prime downtown real estate. His attorney occupied an office on a smaller, but no less prime, parcel a block closer to the ocean. Einstein motored down the gently sloping sidewalk. On a bright day, downtown Santa Barbara dazzled. Today, a winter gloom overshadowed the white stucco buildings, their red tiled roofs the dull hue of dried blood.

A woman exited the office as he approached, and she held the door for him.

Attorney Stan Klingman ushered him into his office. "I'm afraid I don't have good news." He waved Einstein to the conference table, where a chair had been removed to create space for his wheelchair.

Stan fanned files across the table. "On paper," he began, "Winston Rafferty is a pauper. The family flatly rejected any obligation to offer a settlement beyond what their insurance is covering. Their attorneys are prepared to fight us every step of the way and bury us with paperwork. And, frankly, their trusts are so compartmentalized it would take years to unravel."

Einstein rubbed his hand over his heart. "I've got nothing but time."

"Time is expensive." Stan's face pinched. "Which brings me to my next bit of bad news. I agreed to work pro bono for you while exploring the feasibility of a suit. But, considering the difficulty of proving negligence—"

"What if it was intentional?"

"We've discussed this. If the prosecutor thought they could prove Rafferty's intent to harm you, we wouldn't be having this conversation. But the police didn't find anything to suggest it was an intentional act. Surfing is an inherently dangerous sport. At this point, going after Rafferty would be a fool's journey."

"I've been called worse than a fool."

"Yes, but *I'm* a businessman. And, more importantly, I'm a realist."

"What about Rafferty's statements?"

"What about them? You were unconscious. The medic who heard him say he was sorry has suffered an acute case of amnesia."

"Can't we—"

"You're free to contact another attorney, but I'm sorry. There is no *we* anymore."

Einstein had prepared for this moment, but it still left him feeling lightheaded, as if he were pinned under the crush of water, tumbled across the ocean floor and unable to fight his way to the surface.

"I really am sorry, Peter."

Peter.

"I guess that's that, then."

Stan cleared his throat. "You going to be all right?"

For a second, Einstein wondered if Stan's conscience was bothering him, but then he remembered the man was a lawyer, so he probably didn't have one.

"Don't worry," he said. "I'll be fine."

* * *

Lesson Three: Don't Drop in on Someone

In the hospital, a year earlier, there'd been more than enough time for Einstein to think about what had happened. But he'd been unconscious for most of it, which didn't leave him with a lot of details to work with.

Einstein had only seen Winston Rafferty once before that Monday, two or three months earlier. He'd been talking with a student in the parking lot when a Hummer pulled in and straddled two spaces. Rafferty, all highlighted hair and bleached teeth, unloaded a beautiful vintage longboard. He scanned the crowd and swaggered toward Einstein, tucking the board under his arm the wrong way and oblivious to the wax rubbing off on the side of his wetsuit.

Einstein went back to discussing the science of surfing with the teen he was mentoring. "Balance is your friend. Every time you move forward or backward, side to side on your board, you're shifting the downward force of gravity against the upward force of buoyancy."

Rafferty planted himself in front of Einstein. "I want you to teach me how to surf."

"Dude, I'm kind of busy."

"Don't worry, I'll make it worth your while." He posed as if he expected paparazzi to jump from the bushes.

"Look, leave me your number. If I have an opening, I'll call you."

Parentheses formed between the guy's eyebrows. "I'm Winston Rafferty."

Einstein inhaled a long breath through his nose, the kind of breath he'd draw right before catching a particularly gnarly wave. "Winston, was it?" He exhaled. "I don't want to be as rude as you're being, but now's not the time. And certainly not with that board."

Rafferty dropped the tail of the board onto the pavement, and Einstein winced at the guy's disrespect of such a classic piece.

"What's wrong with my board?" Rafferty said. "It's the best money can buy."

"Not for someone who doesn't know jack-shit about surfing."

"I'll double your asking price."

"I don't charge for helping people out, which you'd know if you bothered to ask anyone around here. They'll also tell you that, if I think I can help you, I'll ask if you want some advice. You want to *hire* someone to teach you to surf, there are plenty of people who do that for a living."

"They aren't Peter 'Einstein' Calihan." Rafferty flexed his fingers into a one-handed air quote. "You see, I *have* done my research. You're the best there is around here. I want you. Name your price."

Einstein turned to his student. "Why don't you head down to the water and do some stretches? I'll be there in a couple of minutes."

The teen took off, and Einstein drew another long breath, but this time he didn't hold it. "Let me make myself clear. I share my experience with people I think can actually benefit from it. You can't, because you've already demonstrated that you don't listen."

"You're wrong."

"Argumentative, too." Einstein said. "Okay, Surfing 101. What's a kook?"

"I don't know. A type of board?"

"Not even close. A kook is someone who can't even fathom the depth of their own cluelessness." Einstein softened his voice. "Look, have you even *read* anything about surfing?"

Rafferty shifted his weight. "Of course."

The condescension in those two words confirmed everything Einstein suspected about Winston Rafferty. "Yeah? Explain to me what a pop-up is."

"You're the expert. You tell me."

"It's the maneuver you do at exactly the right moment when you go from lying on the board to standing. You should have been practicing that move all week before even coming out here."

Einstein paced in front of his truck to burn off his aggravation. The guy was a tool, and nothing Einstein said was going to change that. He stopped. "Let me give you some free advice." He pointed to Rafferty's longboard. "You go out on that stick in these waves, and one of two things is going to happen: either you're going to hurt yourself or, worse, you're going to take out someone else. Get a foam board. Something appropriate for a beginner. You'll kill someone with *that* board, and I want no part of it."

Einstein grabbed his own shortboard and jogged toward the path, leaving Rafferty sputtering in the parking lot. In hindsight, maybe that hadn't been a smart move. It had left Rafferty with no doubt about his inadequacy, and a man like Winston Rafferty never liked to dwell on his shortcomings.

Flash forward to the day Einstein's life changed. Winter storms the prior week had created some killer waves, and the period between them had settled into that perfect rhythm that was as steady and flawless as a sleeping baby's breath. The Friday and weekend lineups had been crowded, but there were enough waves for everyone, and, for the most part, everybody minded their manners. By the time Monday rolled around, the crowd had thinned—which meant plenty of room to spread out for the lucky few who could ditch the workday grind.

The clouds had cleared, and the sky was a blue as deep as the ocean. He'd been surfing each of the last three days, so he took frequent breaks. Surfing at the age of fifty-six took more out of him than it had in his younger years.

But it was all good. Every time he hit the ocean he took a moment to reflect. Einstein wasn't religious, not exactly, but, surrounded by water, he was damn grateful. He had his health, a job he did mostly from home, and a girl from Goleta who still made his heart race, as much as catching major air and sticking the landing to ride it on out.

This day, the waves were legendary. The ideal swell started

in the Gulf of Alaska. Born in the ferocity of a storm, it crossed the ocean, gathering strength until it clipped the Hollister Ranch sea shelf, refracted against the Gaviota coast, caressed the shores of Santa Barbara and finally sacrificed itself to a surfer on Rincon Point. On those blessed days, you could catch a wave at the top of the Indicator and ride that sonofabitch past the Rivermouth into the Cove in a run that felt like it went all the way to San Diego. That swell could make a hardened surfer weep.

He paddled outside for a final run. That's when he saw Rafferty, wearing some godawful neon rash guard, on that sweet longboard he had no business riding.

Not even Rafferty could ruin this day, and Einstein gave him his politest bro-nod. Maybe Rafferty didn't see it. Anyway, Rafferty was bobbing even farther outside—which, considering the skill of the guys in the lineup, was actually a smart move.

The afternoon sun started to dip, and Einstein decided to head in and get warm. A nice roller was building, and he paddled, quickening his stroke as the wave built beneath him. He positioned his hands, ready to pop up, then caught motion in his peripheral vision. A searing pain sliced across his lower back. Then he felt nothing at all.

Steve, another surfer, saw the impact and rushed to his aid, dragged him through the surf. All Rafferty did was wring his hands and watch. Someone on the beach filmed the rescue on his phone and uploaded it to YouTube. Steve untangled Einstein's leash and used his surfboard to keep him stable. Then he and three other guys lifted him above the wash and carried him to the beach like sand-encrusted pall bearers.

The short story? Spinal paraplegia.

The longer version included a medically-induced coma, surgery, weird dreams, weirder awakenings, and finally some lucidity. Finger-dexterity tests? Great. Point-his-toes test? Epic fail.

In the hospital, Einstein's wife Sophie sat with him, holding his hand, telling him it'd be all right. Eventually he was transferred to a rehabilitation center for a thirty-day stint, where he had his first up-close-and-personal with his new wheelchair. During the sleepless nights, Einstein learned to surf the web.

Winston Rafferty, he learned, was a party boy with a temper, who grudgingly flew the family flag at local fundraisers. Those who interacted with him described an arrogant know-it-all who really didn't know much of anything and wasn't afraid to prove it.

Lesson Four: Energy Matters

There's a move in surfing called the pivot turn. The tail of the surfboard remains damn near stationary while the rest of the board swings around. Einstein's attorney had made it clear: his legal remedies had been exhausted. So it was time to pivot.

Despite what had happened at Rincon, that was still where Einstein could think the clearest. Not even an asshole like Rafferty could take that away from him. He headed south, his attorney's words haunting him on the drive to the Point.

The demeanor of surfers in the Rincon parking lot changed, depending on the time of day and the season. Dawn-patrol surfers were serious. Even the newbies were out there to rack up hours, not to be paddlepusses and play in the whitewater. On the weekends, it was a free-for-all, more tailgating and posing than splashing. Summer lineups could include over a hundred surfers as kooks swelled the ranks, doing their best to learn a new sport. Winter surfing required braving weather and water temps that didn't go north of sixty. But today was Monday, and most of the surfers would be retired, independently wealthy, or ditching class.

The one he cared about hadn't arrived yet.

Winston Rafferty was a creature of habit, which made things easy for Einstein. Mondays were a given. Wednesdays and Thursdays were possible. Weekends were out: the last time he'd surfed on a Saturday, someone had waxed insults across his Hummer's doors.

Einstein backed into a space, rolled down the windows to catch the breeze, and fired up his laptop.

It was common knowledge Rafferty lived in one of the beachfront McMansions off Padero Lane. Einstein had driven past the house. From the street, there was nothing to see but a twelve-foot wall and a massive gated entry. The house would be a hard nut to crack. Not impossible, but there were easier ways to target Winston Rafferty.

Financially, the Rafferty family trust acted as a huge firewall against legal maneuvers. Winston was the weak link. More accurately, his phone was. He used it for mobile banking, surfing porn sites, and sending lewd texts to his bimbo du jour—and he left it in his Hummer every time he surfed.

Most people don't appreciate the power of technology. But to an IT geek, the air buzzes with secrets. The uninitiated assume those secrets are invisible, safe. They aren't. With a couple of mouse clicks, anyone can find a video explaining how to fake a public Wi-Fi hotspot. From there, it's child's play to hijack transmissions and track data.

If he wanted to, Einstein could make Rafferty miserable. Armed with access to his phone, he could control the asshole's home thermostat, security system, television, doorbell, treadmill, smoke detector, toothbrush, refrigerator, coffee maker, garage door, sprinklers and a handful of other smart appliances. But none of that interested Einstein.

He was following the money.

Most bank apps don't require two-factor authentication. More importantly, most bank apps don't guard against fraudulent security encryption information. Once that's in place, intercepting, tweaking, and relaying information meant to be between client and bank suddenly has another man in the middle. And that opened up a whole host of possibilities not sanctioned by the Rafferty family trust.

Einstein had spent the last several months gathering account numbers, researching routing numbers, identifying beneficiaries, breaking down firewalls, reconstructing faux pathways. He'd done dry runs on his own accounts. Technically, hacking isn't taught at the university, but the skills learned in school are easily adaptable.

What happened next would be up to Rafferty.

It was three o'clock before the Hummer entered the lot and parked across two spots close to the beach access trail. Predictable as always.

Rafferty got out. When he saw Einstein's van, he smiled and waved.

That wasn't in the playbook. Normally Rafferty went out of his way to avoid him. Einstein waved back, using fewer fingers. Childish, maybe, but it was worth it to see Rafferty's wattage dim.

Rafferty drew his cell phone from the pocket of his board shorts and tapped the screen. Had Einstein been interested, he could have opened up a program on his laptop and followed along in real time. But that seemed petty. It was time to move on to more important things.

Rafferty finished what he was doing and tossed his phone into the car. He crossed the lot with his chest thrown forward and shoulders back, as if he were going to throw down the minute he got to the van. Einstein lowered the lid of his laptop.

Rafferty stopped just shy of the van. "No hello for me today?" he said, and then snapped his fingers. "Wait, I forgot. You had a conference with your attorney this morning, didn't you?"

Einstein didn't bother to ask how Rafferty knew. They each had their secrets.

"I'm curious. You going to continue to stand and fight me or walk away?" His mouth twisted into an ugly smile. "Oh, that's right, you can't do either."

"You did it on purpose," Einstein said. "You hit me intentionally."

"I'm sure your attorney has explained to you there's no way you can prove that."

"Doesn't change the facts," Einstein said. "You dropped in on me and purposely ran me over."

Rafferty lifted a shoulder. "Accidents happen."

"I saw a video of you surfing," Einstein said. "I bet you practiced every day from the time I told you no to the day you tried to slice me in half with your board. All that practice and you know what?" He leaned closer, like he wanted to share a secret. "You can stand on the deck, but you still suck."

Rafferty jerked back. "If you didn't have such a stick up your ass, you could have made a lot of money those couple of weeks."

"You surf just like I thought you would." Einstein raised his voice. A few of the surfers in the lot knew their history and moved closer. "No feel for the water. Trying to muscle your way across the waves. Steamrolling everything in your path."

A flush crawled up Rafferty's neck and settled on his face. "I'm glad you didn't drown. How's it feel to know you'll never surf again?"

Einstein had almost added the adaptive surfing organization he'd founded to the list of nonprofits slated to receive an unexpected windfall from Winston Rafferty. But he didn't want anything to even remotely link him to the transfers.

He was itching to click the button and initiate the transfers. That revealed a character flaw in himself that he didn't like, but he took solace in the fact that not once had he wanted to hurt Rafferty physically. A rationalization, sure, but he could live with it. In retrospect, he hadn't enjoyed dissecting Rafferty's life. He'd felt dirtied by the intimacy of it all. That ended today.

Spit had gathered in the corners of Rafferty's mouth. "You're a nobody now." He spun away from the van and waved his hands to get the attention of everyone in the lot. "Hey, guys!" he yelled. "You may not know it, but once upon a time, Einstein here was a surfer!"

Einstein re-opened his laptop, smiled, and pressed Enter. Numbers scrolled across the screen as the wire transfers initiated.

"Oh, I still am," he said.

ACKNOWLEDGMENTS

My thanks to the authors who enthusiastically contributed stories, to Pam Stack and Micki Browning for connecting me with several of the writers, to Eric Campbell and Lance Wright at Down & Out Books for their encouragement...and, most of all, to the incomparable Jimmy Buffett, whose music and lyrics inspired this book.

ABOUT THE CONTRIBUTORS

MICHAEL BRACKEN is a novelist and prolific short-story writer. He has received the Edward D. Hoch Memorial Golden Derringer Award for Lifetime Achievement as well as two additional Derringer Awards. He is the author of the private-eye novel *All White Girls* and several other books. More than 1,200 of his short stories have appeared in *Alfred Hitchcock's Mystery Magazine*, *Ellery Queen's Mystery Magazine*, *The Best American Mystery Stories*, and many other periodicals and anthologies, and he has edited six collections of crime fiction, including *The Eyes of Texas: Private Eyes from the Panhandle to the Piney Woods* and the three-volume *Fedora* series. He lives and writes in Texas. *CrimeFictionWriter.com*

M.E. BROWNING served twenty-two years in law enforcement and retired as a captain before turning to a life of crime fiction. Writing as Micki Browning, she penned the Agatha-nominated and award-winning Mer Cavallo mysteries, and her short stories and nonfiction have appeared in anthologies, magazines, and textbooks. As M.E. Browning, she recently began a new series of Jo Wyatt mysteries with *Shadow Ridge*. Under both names, she is unapologetically sarcastic. *MEBrowning.com*

DON BRUNS is a lifelong Buffett fan who met Jimmy and played tambourine with his pick-up band at the Key West Margaritaville. A former standup comic and advertising executive, he is the author of sixteen mystery/thriller novels, including the

"Stuff" series (about two young friends who start a detective agency in Miami) and a series about a New Orleans cop and a voodoo queen. *DonBrunsBooks.com*

BRUCE ROBERT COFFIN is the author of the award-winning Detective Byron mysteries. As a detective sergeant in the Portland Police Department in Maine, he supervised all homicide and violent-crime investigations; following the terror attacks of September 11, 2001, he spent four years investigating counter-terrorism cases for the FBI and earned the Director's Award, the highest award a non-agent can receive. His short fiction has appeared in a number of anthologies, including *Best American Mystery Stories 2016*. *BruceRobertCoffin.com*

JOHN M. FLOYD has contributed short stories to AHMM, EQMM, *The Strand Magazine*, *The Saturday Evening Post*, and many other publications. Three of his stories have appeared in the annual *Best American Mystery Stories* anthologies, and another was recently optioned for film. He is a four-time Derringer Award winner, an Edgar nominee, a recipient of the Edward D. Hoch Memorial Golden Derringer Award for lifetime achievement, and the author of eight books. *JohnMFloyd.com*

JEFFERY HESS is the author of several novels (*No Salvation, Tushhog, Beachhead*) and a collection of short stories (*Cold War Canoe Club*), and he edited the award-winning *Home of the Brave* anthologies. He served six years aboard Navy ships and was stationed in Pascagoula for a memorable part of that time. He lives in Florida, where he leads the DD-214 Writers' Workshop for military veterans. *JefferyHess.com*

LEIGH LUNDIN started writing in power-outage darkness amid Florida hurricanes. In 2006, his first story "Swamped," won EQMM's Readers Choice Award—the first time a first-time writer took home that prize. He was an original member of *criminalbrief.com* and co-founded *sleuthsayers.org*. He has lived and worked in the US and Canada, Western Europe, and South Africa—but, like a Jimmy Buffett character, aims to wind up somewhere in the Caribbean.

ISABELLA MALDONADO wore a gun and badge in real life before turning to crime writing. The first Latina to attain the rank of captain in the Fairfax County Police Department, she retired as the commander of special investigations and forensics. During her career, her varied assignments included hostage negotiator, department spokesperson, and precinct commander, and she uses her extensive law-enforcement background to bring a realistic edge to her writing. *The Cipher*, the first book in her new series featuring FBI Special Agent Nina Guerrera, was published last year. *IsabellaMaldonado.com*

ALISON McMAHAN is the author of *Alice Guy Blaché, Lost Visionary of the Cinema* (Bloomsbury, 2002) and the YA historical mystery *The Saffron Crocus* (Black Opal, 2014), and has contributed short fiction to anthologies including *The Beat of Black Wings: Crime Fiction Inspired by the Songs of Joni Mitchell* (Untreed Reads, 2020), Sisters in Crime's *Fatally Haunted* (Down & Out, 2019), the Mystery Writers of America's *Scream and Scream Again* (HarperCollins, 2018), and *Busted: Arresting Stories from the Beat* (Level Best, 2017). *AlisonMc-Mahan.com*

LAURA OLES is a photo industry journalist and crime writer. Her debut mystery, *Daughters of Bad Men*, was an Agatha nominee, a Claymore Award finalist and a Killer Nashville Readers' Choice nominee; she is also a Writers' League of Texas Award finalist. Her short stories have appeared in several anthologies, including the Silver Falchion winner *Murder on Wheels* and the 2019 Bouchercon anthology *Denim, Diamonds and Death*. *LauraOles.com*

RICK OLLERMAN is the author of four novels (*Turnabout, Shallow Secrets, Truth Always Kills,* and *Mad Dog Barked*) and a non-fiction collection of essays (*Hardboiled, Noir and Gold Medals: Essays on Crime Fiction Writers from the '50s Through the '90s*). He edits *Down & Out: The Magazine* and has edited several anthologies, including the 2019 Bouchercon collection *Denim, Diamonds & Death. Ollerman.com*

JOSH PACHTER was the 2020 recipient of the Short Mystery Fiction Society's Golden Derringer Award for Lifetime Achievement. In addition to his work as a writer and translator, he edited *The Beat of Black Wings: Crime Fiction Inspired by the Songs of Joni Mitchell* (Untreed Reads) and *The Misadventures of Nero Wolfe* (Mysterious Press) and co-edited *Amsterdam Noir* (Akashic Books) and *The Misadventures of Ellery Queen* (Wildside Press). *JoshPachter.com*

NEIL PLAKCY is the author of the Honolulu-based Mahu Investigations series, a series of gay romances set in South Beach, and other romance and mystery titles. He lives across the Intracoastal waterway from the Margaritaville resort with his husband and two dogs, surrounded by the music of Jimmy Buffett. *MahuBooks.com*

ROBERT J. RANDISI is the founder of the Private Eye Writers of America and the co-founder of Western Fictioneers, and also co-founded *Mystery Scene* magazine. The recipient of lifetime achievement awards in the mystery and Western genres, he is the author of more than six hundred and fifty books (including the Rat Pack, Joe Keough, Miles Jacoby, and Nick Delvecchio series) and the editor of some forty anthologies. His recent titles include *The Headstone Detective Agency* and *Headstone's Folly,* both from Down & Out.

LISSA MARIE REDMOND is a retired cold-case homicide detective from Buffalo, NY. She is the author of the Cold Case Investigation series and *The Secrets They Left Behind*, a standalone thriller; her short fiction has appeared in *Buffalo Noir, Mystery Tribune* and *Down & Out: The Magazine*. She lives in Buffalo with her husband, two kids, an energetic puppy, and an ungrateful cat. *LissaMarieRedmond.com*

ELAINE VIETS is the author of thirty-three bestselling mysteries in four series—the hardboiled Francesca Vierling novels, the traditional Dead-End Job books, the cozy Josie Marcus Mystery Shopper series, and the Angela Richman, Death Investigator, books—and has won the Agatha, Anthony and Lefty Awards. Reviewer Cindy Chow called *A Deal with the Devil and 13 Short Stories* (Crippen & Landru) "a stunning collection." *ElaineViets.com*

BOOKS

On the following pages are a few
more great titles from the
Down & Out Books publishing family.

For a complete list of books and to
sign up for our newsletter,
go to DownAndOutBooks.com.

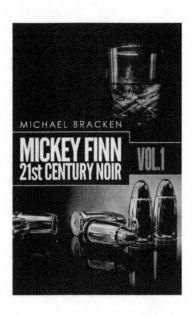

Mickey Finn: 21ˢᵗ Century Noir Vol. 1
Michael Bracken, editor

Down & Out Books
December 2020
978-1-64396-158-3

Mickey Finn: 21st Century Noir is a crime-fiction cocktail that will knock readers into a literary stupor.

Twenty contributors push hard against the boundaries of crime fiction, driving their work into places short crime fiction doesn't often go, into a world where the mean streets seem gentrified by comparison and happy endings are the exception rather than the rule.

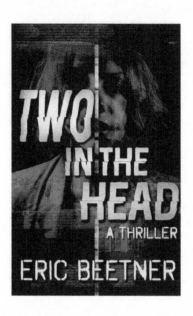

Two in the Head: A Thriller
Eric Beetner

Down & Out Books
January 2021
978-1-64396-170-5

Samantha Whelan is a DEA agent, and not always a straight and narrow one. She's been taking bribes and doing favors for Calder and Rizzo—big players in narco traffic in southern California—for years. She turned down a deal that night, but it meant killing her fiancé, an assistant district attorney. And it meant betraying her DEA brethren more deeply than she had so far. It was too much. So Calder and Rizzo tried to blow her up.

What happened then...she split. Samantha became Samantha and Sam. Two halves of the same person. The good side and the bad side. The two opposing forces living within her for so long were now free to fight it out to see who will win control.

All Due Respect 2020

Chris Rhatigan & David Nemeth, editors

All Due Respect, an imprint of
Down & Out Books
November 2020
978-1-64396-165-1

Twelve short stories from the top writers in crime fiction today.

Featuring the work of Stephen D. Rogers, Tom Leins, Michael Pool, Andrew Davie, Sharon Diane King, Preston Lang, Jay Butkowski, Steven Berry, Craig Francis Coates, Bobby Mathews, Michael Penncavage, and BV Lawson.

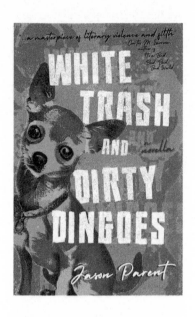

White Trash and Dirty Dingoes
Jason Parent

Shotgun Honey, an imprint of
Down & Out Books
July 2020
978-1-64396-101-9

Gordon thought he'd found the girl of his dreams. But women like Sarah are tough to hang on to.

When she causes the disappearance of a mob boss's priceless Chihuahua, she disappears herself, and the odds Gordon will see his lover again shrivel like nuts in a polar plunge.

With both money and love lost, he's going to have to kill some SOBs to get them back.

Made in the USA
Monee, IL
30 October 2021